Reflections on *Love,*

This insightful book pres..
buried grief and abuse to b..
and, ultimately, accepting that person. She takes those g........ ....
with her feline family, sharing with them as they grow and interact.
When two of her cats pass to the "other place," she is there, helping
them through and realizing, finally, that emotions are okay; they
are natural. It is then that she is able to accept her own feelings
regarding her mother's death many years before. The interaction
between the author and her cats—and among the cats themselves—
fascinated me, as I found this to be a very real family embracing true
familial love. Uplifting!

- Janet Litherland, Author of *Worth Dying For*

For anyone who finds comfort in the unconditional love of animals
and how that love may resonate with our human experiences of loss,
acceptance and appreciation - here is a book written from the heart,
to heal the heart and calm the mind.

- Marlis Jermutus, Author of *From Now to Now*

Bettina came into my life through her love of cats- "fur people".
So it does not surprise me, that her first book 'Love, Always - My
Journey through Grief' would also be about this great love. Her
prose is clean and engaging, her ability to reach into the minds of
her subjects makes this, while sad at times, a wonderful read.

- Kathleen L. Smith , Author of *Defining Grace, Palpitations*

Love, Always is an excellent read and a very enjoyable way to
capture a glimpse of Bettina's life. Following Bettina's story I could
revisit the painful memories caused by my favorite cat Murphy's
tragic death - thus, becoming more tranquil, peaceful and accepting
of his passing.

- Craig Bloch, Founder of *Bloch Piano*

Bettina's close relationships with her beloved cats have produced
cathartic effects in her own human life experiences. These stories
are touching (though some passages are painful to read) and,
ultimately, life affirming. One of the most fortunate human
capacities is the ability to develop deep bonds with animals as
sentient beings.........Inspiring.

- Paula Scoggins, and

Mike Jones, Animal Curator of the *Tallahassee Museum*

Love, Always
My Journey through Grief

by Bettina Maria Krone

pelorian digital

pelorian digital
One Front Street
Leeds, Massachusetts
01053 USA
www.pelorian.com

Book and Cover design by
Bettina Maria Krone & Richard Rasa

ISBN-13:978-1490925554
ISBN-10:1490925554

Love, Always
My Journey through Grief

by Bettina Maria Krone

Contents

Introduction

Omi, my grandmother, gave me my first diary. Omi said she and her daughter both enjoyed journaling, recording life's events and the emotions associated with them. For me writing is a way of processing life, something external, putting my thoughts on paper, reflecting on what's happening. I even wrote an entire journal just for Mammi, my mother, for the funeral I made for her in March of 2010. I was six years old when Mammi died forty-five years earlier.

The grief over her death remained with me through all those years.

In August of 2010, as my cat friends Carmelita and Amber fell ill, I needed to journal every day about my emotions and revisit the grief over Mammi's death. I felt I had to accompany my cats on their dying journey while celebrating their lives and mine. I had to embrace death and the circle of life, finally going into my mourning all the way. It is not all about sorrow – there are cute cat stories in here and I tell about positive thoughts and experiences which helped me on my travels.

My native language is German, hence the German references and perhaps here and there a German undercurrent is noticeable. My story continues, as I am moving on in my journey, so it is best to read the book from front to back.

Since we are all connected, most of my friends I want to thank are already mentioned in my book! I like that! They are in my life and part of it and helped me during the time I write about in this book and always.

Thank you all so many times for your knowledge, love and support: Dr. Otfried Guhrt, Paula Scoggins and Mike Jones, Bob Johnson and the Jungian Group, Velma Frye and her singing circle, Sharon Callahan, Rita Reynolds, Barbara Schmitz, Sally Malloy, Maria and Mischa Steurer, Kathy L. Smith and Marlis Jermutus.

It is always a long way from writing a book, the first draft, to reaching the final version – Tim Morrison of Write Choice Services, was instrumental in helping 'Love, Always' during that process. Thank you, Tim, for all the editing and helpful suggestions along the way.

Special thanks go to Paula and Mike, Kathy and Marlis for their helpful reviews about my book. And to Jennifer Clinard and Marlis who gave me thought- and artful suggestions for the cover.

Meanwhile, there are new friends or friends who have resurfaced in my life, like Janet Litherland, who wrote such a lovely review for me – thank you, Janet.

A new friend of mine is Craig Bloch. I thank you, Craig, for your love and the nice review you wrote for my book.

Now, as I write these thank you notes, Love, Always is already out there, getting formatted and put together for printing: for all that my big thanks go to Richard Rasa for making the publication process so easy, and getting the computers to cooperate and all. That is a huge help, thank you, Rasa!

As you visit the stories about my sorrow, I wish for you to feel held by what I have written and being enveloped by my words like a blanket, or climb upon my words like a magic carpet to ride through the land of grief.

Enjoy reading my book! I wish you a fulfilled and happy life!

Love, Always

My Journey through Grief

Chapter 1

My Journey Begins

The Funeral

The second funeral for my mother in March of 2010 was a nice and quiet one. I was the only one present; that was just the way I had wanted it. This time.

We had spent her last days together. I told her about my wishes and thoughts and ideas and I read parts of my journal to her, the parts where I had written about the trauma I had experienced after her death in 1965. It felt good to be able to bring that deep grief into the open and share it with her.

I bought her a present. I cried a lot. I listened to music; I think she really liked *Swan Lake* by Tchaikovsky. I read poetry to her, and I talked with her about us and life and death and everything in between. I never left her side during her last night.

I chose spring flowers for her funeral and arranged them into a simple, elegant bouquet. On the glittery-silver bow it said "With eternal love/in ewiger liebe – go in peace/gehe in frieden – Deine tochter B.M./your daughter B.M" written by me. The cd-player provided classical music by Tchaikovsky, Telemann and Mozart. The celebration was very festive as well as sad.

There was no wake. Nobody needed to be notified. No will needed to be read. This time, in 2010, there was no body and no grave.

The Trauma

In one of my favorite magazines *Brigitte Woman*[1] Nadine Barth describes in her article "Das Haus meiner Mutter" = "My Mother's House" how her mother kept remodeling and rearranging the childhood house for forty years (I translate):

"I know her paths. Her paths through the house. Her paths through the garden. It is a secret latticework, with all its winding ways like stories in a thick volume. It is her world that she created and developed further, adding more facets along the way."

I love the way Nadine writes about her mother's paths. It seems to be a metaphor for life in general.

I do not know any paths of my mother. I do not remember Mammi; how she might have made paths. I do not remember our time together at all. Mammi will never be here. I never had, I never will have, a conversation with her as a grown woman, from friend to friend. I will never hear what she would have told me about life, what her experiences were. I do not even know whether she liked cats or what her favorite color was or if she enjoyed drinking coffee as much as I do. I will never know her dreams, her desires. I will never know who she was.

My mother, whom I called *Mammi*, was born in Berlin in 1933 into a world of earthshattering political turmoil, on the eve of horrific crimes and a mad, stupid war to come. My father was born in Berlin fourteen years earlier right at the end of another devastating war. While still in school, he was thrown into the crazed battle of the Second World War. For six years he was held as a prisoner of war in Russia. He never talks about that time; I cannot even imagine the nightmare he must have lived through.

My father eventually came back home to Berlin and in 1956 he married our mother, whom I think he loved very deeply. I arrived two years later. And then, a few months after giving birth to my last sibling, Mammi died from leukemia. At that time, there was no treatment for cancer.

I was not allowed to see her or say good-bye to her. In 1965, as a six year old child, I was not even allowed to attend her funeral.

After my mother's death I felt fear for the first time that I remember. I was fearful of people breaking into the house at night, of the dark, of bad things happening, fearful of life itself. Mammi would never come back. The hole she left inside of me, in my life, could never be filled again. A part of me died with Mammi in 1965; the part that believed life to be okay.

Left with three young children, half a year after Mammi's death our father married a woman who neither was a match for him nor us. All during our upbringing we three children had to deal with all kinds of abuse: physical, emotional, verbal and psychological.

The death of one's mother is the most traumatic event that can happen to a young child. Mammi was torn out of my life. Irreplaceable. Back in 1965 and the years after, nobody in my family really was aware of what was going on with me. Apparently I did not talk about it so my relatives thought I was fine. How could I have been fine? I had experienced a tremendous shock and trauma. Mammi's death shook me to my core.

I did feel like an outcast, I felt there must be something wrong with me because I did not have a mother. Sometime in the Eighties I found the book *Motherless Daughters*[2] by Hope Edelman. Reading it was like a revelation to me: Hope writes about all the false beliefs, the "magical thinking," I had held for so long about guilt and inadequacy, not belonging, weirdness, not-okayness and the thoughts that I absolutely could have done something to prevent Mammi's death. While working through that book I was able to move through an important cycle of my grief. But that happened many years later.

After Mammi's death, the world and life itself remained a fearful place for me, reinforced through the dysfunctional upbringing that followed, an environment in that I always felt unsafe and uncared for.

I missed Mammi terribly, every day of my life.

The Grief

Not a day went by during my childhood and puberty where I did not long for Mammi. I grieved deeply for her, every day. I fantasized how it would be like if she would be alive and with us three children. Everything, life itself, would surely be okay then.

I so needed Mammi during those years. Life was not okay for me. I did not feel okay. I continued to believe there was something wrong with me and that I did not belong, that became even more pronounced once I had started school - I did not have a mother but all the other kids did. Furthermore at my parents' house nobody was there for me at all.

Weighed down by guilt and grief I absolutely did think I could have done – or not done - something to prevent Mammi's death. I might have resented my baby siblings because I no longer had Mammi all to myself. I felt that perhaps I got punished now by Mammi's dying for thinking these 'bad' thoughts. I felt guilty for not being able to bring Mammi back because I should have died instead. I felt guilty that I could not make life right for Papa. And I felt guilty and ashamed that I was so angry and furious at Mammi for having left us. I had rage attacks where I would throw stuff around and banged doors and screamed at my siblings. I felt guilty just because I was alive and Mammi was not. I felt guilty that so often I was not able to make life right for my little siblings and prevent the abuse of being hit, severely scolded or being locked in a dark room that was happening to my younger siblings. I am only five years older, so back then I was barely eight, nine years old.

Back then I also believed I had to behave in a perfect way and be in control of everything, so nothing bad would happen again. I had to be perfect, so life would be okay. I had to be perfect, so nobody would abandon me again. I had to be perfect, to pay for my badness that made Mammi leave. I tried to make sure people – family, friends, and strangers – would all like me; better yet; love me. I continued to mostly live life how I should be, what I should do. In short: I tried to be so good that no one would want to leave me again. Ever.

It was a tall order for a little girl. As a child, it was not a conscious decision. I did not have words or even thoughts about all the emotions that flooded my daily life. I had no choice but to survive. So I learned how to sense, to intuit, all the adults around me to make sure I did not get hurt so often, or to prevent the next incident of abuse. I had to be alert at all times, to brace myself and to protect my siblings for what could happen; hyper vigilance is the word for that. I just had to make sure everything in my life was right; I did not listen to myself, to my needs and wishes; thereby losing my sense for my own wellbeing and self-care in the process. Most often I was not even able to find out what I wanted in the first place, least of all say my wishes or opinions out loud or dare act upon them!

That was the price I paid for the perfectionism and being 'in control.'

While trying to anticipate the next abuse, I could not do the grieving since there was no safe place for me to do that. I lived every day as a balancing act among my unresolved grief, anger, fury and deep sadness.

The Well

As soon as I turned eighteen I left my father's house even though I felt guilty – once again - about not being there for my siblings anymore. By then, however, they were old enough to speak up for themselves.

I attended a vocational school and finished an apprenticeship and in my early twenties I moved into a commune. Two or three other people lived there as well as a clowder of five cats. This environment was a whole new experience for me; there were always people around. We laughed and danced and had discussions and argued and went out together and cooked meals and just spent time together. I only took the occasional job (which was easy to do in the early Eighties), to have enough money to get by, that gave me a lot of free time. I dated a lot - plenty of young men were available.

And then, one day, after a break-up, I found myself drowning, drowning in a deep, deep well of sadness and desperation. I could not even see the light at the top anymore. I was shrouded in darkness, unable to do anything but sit on the sofa. I had trouble breathing; there was no – psychological – air left. Death, despair, hopelessness took a hold of my mind, my body and my spirit.

That was my wake-up call; I needed and wanted therapeutic help. A long journey of healing and finding my life started then.

While in the well, no human being could reach me; I would just stare at anyone who tried to talk with me. Only much later I realized there were beings who did reach me: there was always, day or night, a cat with me. The cats took turns, so one of them would be on my lap, beside me on the sofa or nearby sleeping – the cats never left me alone. My lifelong connection with the furry goddesses and gods started at that time.

I have shared my life with cats ever since.

Mammi with me, Bettina

Me, Bettina, in 1962

Chapter 2

Carmelita

Carmelita and the Furry Gang

My cats are my friends, they are not children. Sure, I provide for them, feed them, clean litter boxes, and take them to the veterinarian – other than that, I let them live their lives the way they want to.

I also take great care in naming my cats. I believe cats – really all animals who come in contact with humans – should receive a name they can live up to, fill in and be proud of.

Friends enjoy each other's company, share their experiences, love and care for each other, and spend time together. The cats and I are doing exactly that. I learn from them. They make me smile – they have been my therapy-cats ever since they cared for me when I was lost in that well of despair more than thirty years ago.

Now I share my life with black and white Artus TopCat. He takes on a lot of responsibility. He checks everything out, patrols the yard; he is just present. On top of that, he takes his job seriously; so much so that I oftentimes talk with him to let him know he can relax more. He is a sweet cat; an old soul, whom I bonded with. He is my forever cat, my lover cat.

Orange-colored Amber Lionqueen is a regal cat, a true lion queen! She is opinionated – she knows what she wants and asks for it. She is truly her own cat. Amber is so beautiful and poised; I call her "my photo model cat!" She demonstrates the "perfect jump" or "how to climb a tree" – these kinds of poses.

Amber is also my watch cat – she starts growling when a car arrives that she does not know. She is friends with Blackie; they groom each other and sleep side by side.

All-black, longhaired Blackie Puschelpaw, the comedian, is sweet with all the cats, especially with Amber Lionqueen. He does not have a mean bone in his body. However, he thinks all humans are boogie people, and they are out to get him. He is sweet with me, but only up to a degree. Hasty movements, loud, unexpected noises, and off he runs; if I so much as think about putting that flea stuff on him (which really only takes about a second!), he disappears.

I rescued Amber and Artus from the local shelter. Blackie was born feral; he decided to move in with me on his own. Then a fourth, tortoiseshell-colored cat arrived at my house.

The little cat was thin, almost to the point of being emaciated. Her coat looked ragged. At first I thought she might belong to someone, so I called around, put an ad in the paper – but nobody ever called about her. I named her Carmelita, this name goes well with her black and brown coat colors.

Over the years they all learned to get along just fine. We have a good life, the five of us. And most important of all, my cats know I always have a limitless supply of love for them.

Carmelita's Diagnosis

"It's about the size of a walnut," Dr. G, the veterinarian, points to the x-ray. I see it, "so in the lung all that dark is good, how it is supposed to be?" I ask. Dr. G nods, "Yes, that's air; it comes out black on the x-ray." I am still holding Carmelita in my arms. It is her chest x-ray we are looking at. "Not good," Dr. G says, "that looks like cancer." I had brought her to the clinic because she has a persistent cough, sometimes three, four times a day, and it lasts a while too. And she is old. We have no idea about her actual age. Five years ago, in September of 2003, when she arrived, Dr. G guessed her to be about fifteen years old.

I held her during the x-rays; the doctor did not want to sedate her because of her age. He just injected her with a little bit of something to take the edge off. The technician and I managed just fine. Dr. G suggested that I could try Prednisone for the cancer. Prednisone is a steroid and helps by reducing inflammation in the body. He gave her an injection and said to call him on Monday to let him know if she was coughing. "If she is fine then," he said, "it is cancer."

Carmelita already gets daily transdermal medication for her thyroid condition that I can just rub in her ear, easy, no fuss. The Prednisone comes as such a cream as well. There is no way I will give her oral medications – she will run away from me after the second time, and I will not frighten her by chasing her around the house.

Finally, after more than an hour at the clinic, we left. Back in her carrier she is happy again. Her paw hangs out the door of the carrier; she rubs her head at the wire-door. She knows we are going home.

Every time we have to go to a veterinarian, Carmelita curls up into a tight ball and clings to me as close as possible. Sometimes it is difficult to distinguish where she ends and I begin. She loses so much hair. Cats shed when they are anxious, afraid, scared. Carmelita sticks her head under my arm. The invisible cat; she says, "If I can't see you, you can't see me either, right?" Not so, Sweetie.

I am quiet on the way home.

We have shared so much together; there was a lot of life happening for me. I got a divorce, had several romantic relationships, moved to Taos, NM, and back to Tallahassee, traveled a lot, worked for my non-profit organization "Cat Life Foundation," attended college, dealt with the onset of menopause, had some health challenges, took care of the cats, dealt with the houses I lived in, redecorated, lived, photographed, wrote, had fun – and the most important of all – learned a huge lot about myself through the Jungian process group I participate in.

Carmelita has led an equally full life – much more challenging for her physically. She had to have x-rays taken several times. She went through surgery for her thyroid for which she is on the transdermal medication now. When she arrived at my house five years ago she came with an old back injury that left her incontinent. She received acupuncture and chiropractic treatment for that. She moved twice across the country with me and the other three cats. It seems she has become deaf now as well.

Through all that she had to endure, she just kept on living and enjoying her life. She is and has been a courageous, marvelous little cat. Not once did I hear her whine or complain about her condition. She shows such dignity, taking each moment with stride and joy by being present and making the most of it.

At home, Carmelita is eager to get out of the carrier. She staggers away and hides under the shelf. She always hides after we return from the vet. The trauma of a medical exam or procedure is just too much for her. She is afraid; she assumes there could be more. She has mistrust in me and the world. It takes Carmelita several hours to come out again. I do pet her and talk to her. That is okay. Then she sits. She sits – upright – by the door and under the table and beside the ottoman. No sleep.

Usually she is sleeping on top of the ottoman; she sleeps a lot these days. I made sure she ate all the food. Now she sits again by the kitchen door. She is alert, her head goes around. No coughing. Not a beep.

After that weekend, we started her on the Prednisone.

It is cancer.

Carmelita Gets Older

Carmelita adjusted well to the Prednisone. She has lived with the cancer diagnosis now for more than two years.

The other day she cried a little when I cut off her fur. It was all matted on her belly. I felt sorry that I had not noticed it sooner – that she obviously cannot clean herself properly anymore. I did cut the fur real slow, I held her, rubbed her head – I let her tuck her head into my hand, she likes that. I gave her time. Afterwards, she hid under the chaise – but for cheese, she came out – she loves that treat. Her favorite is Gruyere-cheese. She can even ask for it: "yere, yere!" She cries. Then she jumped back up on top of the chaise and purred and purred. I brushed her some more – she loses so much hair; it is enough to make another cat out of! I do have the impression she is grateful. I am sure she feels better. After all, cats are always so fastidious about grooming themselves. Perhaps the matted fur was scratching her. Grooming each other or being groomed by a human feels bonding for cats, which is nice. The next morning I brushed her again – I will make a routine for her. Even though cats are so independent and so into doing their own thing, they also love routines and rituals, like being groomed at a certain time, or having playtimes in the evening. Rituals feel comfortable and bonding, I can relate to that.

Carmelita is amazing in how she handles herself! She asks for what she wants – in no uncertain terms "now, now" she says. In the morning she climbs on my bed and squawks in my ear (it does not sound like meow at all) and butts her head in the pillow. FOOD, she says. She can become impatient with me if I ignore her too long.

She keeps to herself; the other cats do harass her occasionally. They sniff her fur; they must smell she is not healthy. They do – at least Blackie and sometimes Artus – wash her head. She loves to have her head rubbed. If someone should stroke her back she squeals – sounds like a warning that it might hurt her. She does not hiss or bite, ever. Often she would sit outside in the sun on the deck like a little old lady saying "I heard sun is good for me!"

She does what she can for herself, even if she falls over while cleaning her body. Or if she has to throw up (which often is a side effect of the thyroid medication) – it is what is happening. No need to feel guilty about it, she says. She remains her poised cat-self; she was and is always true to herself. All the challenges that come with old age – she takes them in stride. I tell my friends about how amazing she is - how humans could learn from her!

Seeing her, observing her humbles me. How dear and loving she remains despite all that she is going through. There is no hissing, no fussing; she is her sweet self. I tell her often how much I love and admire her.

Carmelita is getting ready to leave

It is August now, in 2010. The cancer, combined with old age, finally takes its toll on Carmelita.

Every time I pet her, she purrs – like she always did. Because she is so thin now her purr rumbles even louder! She still likes to have her head rubbed. Now I can pet her all over her body, give her a little massage – which she did not like previously. She seems to enjoy my touch. She is still itchy when I touch her paws – lots of cats do not like that.

I feel so much closer to her, shower her with love, respect her and let her be. I will accompany her to the end. Two years ago, after she had been diagnosed with cancer, I promised her I would not go back to the doctor with her. I will keep my promise. I sense Carmelita wants to see her life through in her own time – I am letting her do that. She so enjoys life; she has had good years with me and the fur-gang. I think she wants to savor every minute she has left.

Carmelita has not eaten since Monday. Today is Friday.

Her body has changed during the past week: aside from being even thinner than before, her flanks have fallen in more. Her belly and chest area are kind of rounded now. She wobbles out of the little hut I had bought for her and staggers into the kitchen that is the adjacent room. My little ancient cat needs lots of breaks on the way. She stands or plops down to catch her breath – until she finally arrives at the water dish. Once there it takes her several minutes to lap some water before she very slowly, resting every other step, enters her safe place again, the hut.

I put a small dish with water right beside the hut – Amber drinks from it to demonstrate to Carmelita what the dish is for. Carmelita leaves the hut and checks it out for herself.

Artus TopCat, Amber Lionqueen and Blackie Puschelpaw, they all know. They observe the little tortoiseshell cat. They let her be.

Yesterday Artus helped Carmelita with the large water bowl in the kitchen. He sniffed her side and nudged her head a bit.

Carmelita still musters up the strength to stagger into the kitchen. I do not know whether she forgets that there is a water dish by her hut or whether she just wants to get out of there.

Artus is on my lap while I write. Amber and Blackie have left the building – they are probably outside on the swing. They love that thing!

And I? Where am I?

I can feel a lot of resistance right now; I am uncomfortable in my skin. It is the resistance to deal with Carmelita's upcoming death; resistance to re-visit my grief over Mammi's death that still lingers. The funeral I had made for Mammi in March brought all my emotions back to the surface. I am processing them, but I feel resistance to deal with all the residual grief, with a new cycle of grieving.

I left the house for an appointment today and I ran some errands. While driving around I caught myself thinking about not wanting to go there, not wanting to go into the grief of losing Carmelita. I resisted being here in the moment, with her. Instead, I occupied myself with external stuff – as I so often do. I do that to avoid facing my emotions, facing my Self.

I finally start crying which is good. I do know Carmelita wants to do this on her own. I respect that. She is peaceful and she has stopped coughing.

After I came back from my round of errands I noticed a change: Carmelita has gotten weaker. And I think I detected the smell --- the smell of a dying cat, a little sour, a little urine, a touch of decay.

Carmelita is still drinking, and I saw her pee on the carpet.

Carmelita's Last Day

My beloved "lucky clover leaf" of cats was with me for seven years. I am grateful for that. It is a long time.

Carmelita purrs. Cats do that for themselves too when they are not feeling well. It is comforting to them as well I suppose. I observe the little tortoiseshell cat, I help her, I am with her. I just pay attention to the present moment, and I do not get distracted.

I have witnessed an animal's death many times. I have, however, never experienced a natural death of a loved one. All my previous cats were euthanized, that is a very different experience all together.

What does Carmelita want? She has been through so much; I think she wants to know I am with her. I forget she is deaf. I just keep talking to her, tell her all that matters: that I love her and wish her a good journey. I give her thanks for all the years. I look in on her every ten or fifteen minutes, pet her, tell her something. She has already crossed over a little bit; she has been spacey for a while now. Carmelita is peaceful in her hut. It looks like she is getting weaker by the hour. This is all I can do, giving her comfort.

The day has remained overcast; it has just 82, 83 degrees Fahrenheit's. The crickets and other insects are at it. There is constant noise outside. I have the screen door closed. Amber and Blackie are on the deck, I do not know where Artus is, upstairs perhaps, in my studio.

Oh, I hear Blackie jumping down from the chair: "brr, brrp," he goes; something like that. He always emits sound bites when he does something physical, it's very cute.

Carmelita has her eyes closed. She sure deserves to leave this earth humble and peaceful and dignified. I feel so very sad for her. It makes me heartbroken to see Carmelita like this and not be able to do more for her. She seems to be quite out of it now. She tried to get up and just fell over. I held the water for her, just one quick lick she took (I do not even know if she got any liquid) and she fell on her side again.

It is heartbreaking; my belly is all cramped up.

Carmelita's Last Evening

Paula and Mike came over and brought dinner. That was so nice of them. Mike is the animal curator here at the Tallahassee Museum. At first we just worked together through my non-profit organization "Cat Life Foundation." Over time I met his wife and the three of us have become close friends.

They both agreed about Carmelita looking peaceful and that she knows how to do this dying thing. They confirmed I have done everything for her; she has had a great seven years. Thank you, my friends, for saying that. I accept it, I take it in.

Mike told me he had often observed that in the last hours or days leading to the death, the breathing does get labored; the medical term for that is agonal breathing. Since I had never been with anyone at a life's natural end, I do not know 'how dying goes.'

I send out ribbons of love to my little cat. I hope she can hold onto them to complete her journey in this life, to cross over the Rainbow Bridge.

Right now, she is in the guest room behind the futon. It is amazing what strength she has left in her; that is a long way from her hut in the corner, here in the sitting area.

Carmelita's Last Night

The world just seems to stop, life comes to a standstill for me when one of my cats is sick or lies dying. It is a place between the worlds. I am at the threshold with them. I accompany them, helping them as much as I can. It is a sacred place. It is a place where we will all be one day. I think it is an honor to be there for somebody during that time. I cannot help but feel very open and very vulnerable, really raw emotionally.

I have to face the grief again; this time with full awareness. I am an adult now; I am not a child anymore having had to deal with my mother's death. It is hard and so very sad to see a loved one go but it is also such a loving time, to be able to say goodbye, to give comfort and safety. I open my heart. I allow myself to feel.

Carmelita has crawled farther behind the futon. It stands in a corner and has a high back leaning against the wall, so there is a good sized dark space behind it. I do not know if she will come out again, I let her be. Whenever I check on her, I stay for a while and talk with her and send her love.

Carmelita did come back out; she sat in front of the water bowl again, did a half-hearted sip and went into the office, underneath the printer table.

All the cats came inside. They all looked around. They know what is going on with Carmelita. Artus sits beside me on the sofa; I am trying to watch a movie which is not working very well. I keep thinking about the little tortoiseshell. It is wet outside; Amber and Blackie might stay in overnight.

At two a.m. Carmelita is still under the printer table. She is still breathing, somewhat labored but she appears peaceful. All the cats have remained inside. That is good.

I go to bed, setting the timer for every half hour. The first time

I checked Carmelita had just moved to another place in the office. The second time she was still in the same spot. And then – I was up and ran into the office before I even knew what was going on, the timer had not gone off. Carmelita just tumbled out from behind the table. She started crying right then – I was there.

I do not know if I had heard something, if it was my intuition, if she had somehow reached out to me that made me run over. It is what I wanted, to be with her in her last moments.

She died at four thirty a.m. I was with her.

I am still so shaken. She cried out a few times, it sounded like groaning. She had some mild seizures, gas and liquid came out of her body; she cried once again and was gone. Her head twitched a few times afterwards. I talked to her, held her, wished her a good journey over the Rainbow Bridge, told her I love her and that I am right here.

I screamed. I let the grief out. My screams carried her spirit, released her. I had gathered her body in my arms and I cried and cried. Finally I could hold her like this; she never wanted to be in my arms or on my lap when she was alive.

Death is so powerful; it goes so deep, into one's Self really. I felt this death so much more powerful since it was a natural death. What do we know about dying – whether it be humans or animals? Perhaps these last hours are important somehow.

I walked around the house with her body for quite a while, crying, getting it out. Later, I found a box and a towel to wrap her body in. A friend will come over in the morning, we will bury her then.

Artus sniffed at her body. His job as TopCat requires that he has to know exactly what is going on around here. Blackie ran away saying he does not want to deal with that, he knows she is not here anymore. Amber was sleepy and not interested. She did not get along well anyway with Carmelita when she was still alive. They all knew, they all had sniffed the little cat and around the places in the house where Carmelita had been.

I let Carmelita, my beloved little tortoiseshell cat, do it her way. Death is so very primal and violent and powerful and emotional.

Carmelita Cat

Artus Topcat

Artus Topcat, a portrait

Amber Lionqueen

Blackie Puschelpaw

Amber, Carmelita, Blackie and Artus outside

Blackie, Artus, Amber and Carmelita on the deck

Chapter 3

Love Lessons

My Heart Hurts So

For a moment there, I thought I needed to tend to Carmelita - I just saw her out of the corner of my eye.

At night I heard the cats; Artus was running around the house, scratching here and there. It was his way of working through Carmelita's passing. He got the areas all cleaned up in his cat world – that is beneficial for me as well. Cats are very good at working in the spiritual realm.

At the moment, I am just dazed; it will take me a long time to process Carmelita's passing. That last night was heavy. What a courageous, amazing little cat! She knew that my home is, was and always will be a good and safe place for her and my other cat-friends. Here it is all about love and respect. I do think that is why she lived with me as long as she did. Why did she choose to die now?

Her death will help me go ever more into my grief for Mammi, by witnessing a loved one's passing. Carmelita gave me the gift to have the experience of being with her in the last minutes of her life on earth. She needed to live out her life until the last breath for her own life experience. Mammi died alone, in the hospital. Did she awake before she crossed over? Or did she just slide over during her sleep? There will never be answers to these questions. I feel humbled and grateful that I could accompany Carmelita on her way out of this realm.

It is a beautiful Sunday morning. The cicadas are giving their concert. The sun is out. It is eighty degrees Fahrenheit. I just saw a hummingbird hovering above the stairs to the deck. It is the first time I have seen one this year! I will put the feeder outside in a few moments. Perhaps Carmelita asked her (or him) to say hello to me?!

Artus is on my lap. We are doing a lot of bonding these days. A dove just landed on the deck-railing. Amber and Blackie, who are outside, went into alert-mode. Now Artus sees the bird – he stalks outside. Of course, the bird is long gone having seen all that movement. Now it is washing-on-the-deck-time. Everybody picks a sunny spot and gives her- or himself a thorough bath. Blackie has to move into the shadow soon – with his all black coat he heats up in no time. Artus is washing his belly which is white, so he enjoys the sunlight.

And I just sit and write and let the grief surface.

Hopelessness

A part of me, my little girl part, once again feels utterly alone in the world; a loved one has died and left me. It feels like a rug has been ripped out from under me, leaving me adrift in anchorless, colorless nothingness. This part of me always feels that way; this "nothing place" stays with me always.

I am going in all the way this time, into the nothingness, into the well. Back then, in 1981, I was in that well for days and days before I could glimpse a little light at the top. I was not even frightened; I was just gone, lost in the darkness of hopelessness and death.

It took me until now to realize that this hopelessness, this desperation and 'death'-like feeling, infiltrates everything. I feel empty inside. I feel there is no hope anywhere, and nothing makes sense. I do not really think that, it is a feeling of – the well of sadness and despair again. I am used to living my life teetering on the rim of the well, always in danger of falling back in. I do not know how life would be without that feeling; I could even say I am scared to find out. I do not know how to get rid of this quiet, deep desperation, how to make the emptiness go away. It is a bottomless sadness, an abyss of dark emptiness.

This hopelessness-complex, or behavior pattern, started when the little girl I was when Mammi died felt deep despair and immeasurable grief. I was always alone. I always had to deal with life by myself. A part of me got stuck in March of 1965 when Mammi died. Nobody was there to help me work through all those frightening emotions. Since I was not allowed to grieve openly and express myself, all those emotions associated with the five stages of grief (anger, denial, bargaining, disorganization, acceptance) were buried inside of me.

All the hurt and anger and fury and grief and negativity I had stuffed away formed a shadow-complex, a behavior pattern. This shadow part often told me what I should or should not do, how to behave, basically how to live my life – with misery and no joy. All those negative beliefs fed the shadow part of me, which feels kind of like a black and dark sponge, soaking up joy and positive energy. Every time I felt inadequate or wrong or somehow not up to par, that shadow part sucked it in and added it to that complex, this behavior pattern. Every time someone told me you don't get it, you're stupid, lazy, useless, worthless and bad; the shadow complex was delighted to have more ammunition to shoot at me. It just kept collecting and sucking up all the negativity I encountered through the abuse following my father's remarrying. As I grew older and moved out of my parents' house, the shadow continued to feed and soak up negative beliefs: every time I thought something that put me down in any way - you look fat or you'll never get that or you have to do x first – it all added to the negativity. When I was a child, this complex was actually helpful in protecting me by separating the misery I felt from my everyday life. I projected all the pain and the grief and the rage on that shadow-part. I felt not safe enough to deal with these emotions back then.

I am beginning to learn how to handle that part of me that feels so sad and overwhelmed, even though it is scary. I do not know how to do life without all that negativity holding me down. There is not much room left for any kind of positive mothering or even praise.

Now I can finally acknowledge the little girl inside of me, the part that got stuck as a six-year-old: she is still so very afraid of – everything, really. She feels lost and alone. She is angry, furious even at Mammi for leaving. And she is angry at the world, at life itself, because she has to deal with all that grief and rage and hurt. And I am angry at myself because I still feel this way. I, as the adult Bettina, finally embrace the little girl inside of me. I let her be, I accept her.

I know that in order to have arrived at this moment, I needed to experience all that I did and live through everything that happened in my life. I would probably not even be here in the U.S., if not for Mammi's death and my subsequent life experiences; after all, all my encounters have made me into the person I am today. I am beginning to feel a deep love and compassion for myself and appreciation for the process, the spiral of life.

Through Carmelita's death I was able to feel life in the moment and go into another round of the life and death spiral. The cats show me every day how to value the little moments and the friendships I have. With the cats, I feel the interconnectedness of all life on our planet.

The Jungian Group

A few years ago I joined a group where we talk about our dreams and our everyday problems with life and the people in it. Bob, the leader, who is a Jungian analyst, emphasizes that his groups are about one's individuation process.

According to the teachings of Carl Gustav Jung, the famous Swiss psychologist, being individuated means to live the life that is truly mine. Living one's life is not about making it right for others or adhering to social protocol; it is about finding out about me – and, during the process – getting rid of all the complexes, the behavior patterns, that repress me on my unique life-path. The individuation process is about finding my balance.

The Jungian teachings including the idea of individuation make a whole lot of sense to me, since they represent what I have always been looking for: my truth. I have been a seeker for as long as I can remember. It is like the spiral of life and death. I go ever deeper inside myself and dig up these challenges I have had to face. One complex after the other I am able to grasp and drag into the light, into consciousness, so that I can deal with them.

It is the cycle of life: we move through life, dealing with the same issues all the time – they come up again and again, until we have resolved them on all levels. Grieving for Mammi and now for Carmelita is a good example of this spiral; I do work on different parts of the grieving process. The more we dig, the deeper we dig, the more stuff comes up, until we might latch on to familial grief and unresolved issues that our relatives carried with them. I understand my parents better now. I am able to make peace with them. I love them. They did their best. I see and understand what Mammi and Papa and even the stepmother, went through during their childhoods. How deep their pain and grief must have been for all they had to endure. Children pick up energies easily, on an unconscious level. They do not even realize yet what is going on in the outside world, they just pick up the vibrations from everywhere. Children are well tuned in to the collective unconscious, not yet tainted and broken through life's pressures, be it through parental, social or cultural influences. The collective unconscious represents our connection to all life. Everything is stored there; it is available to all living beings.

In group we unearthed all the beliefs I have held, all the negativity I grew up with and the resulting self-negating beliefs originating during all the years of abuse I lived through. In group, we did talk about my magical thinking regarding my mother's death. I realized I live my life like I am still waiting for Mammi to return, so that I can start living and enjoying life, that she then would somehow magically give me permission to do so. I want her unconditional love back. I long for her to let me know that I am okay and life is too.

Emotions

Carmelita's death taught me to experience the moment: to live with my emotions in that moment; to take them in, acknowledge and respect them. Fully.

I let myself feel compassion and loving kindness toward myself – for the first time ever. I have never experienced this openness, this vulnerability before – it felt too unsafe or I was ashamed to show a vulnerable side of me. Now I accept the way I feel. I do not try to suppress it or hide it. I recognize it and live it. I let it be part of me. I embrace it as part of me.

I act with my emotions, not against them. I let them happen.

In my family, expressing any kind of emotion was not fashionable. Nobody ever said "I love you" and letting others see one's tears was considered a weakness. I find it difficult to show my emotions for others and to accept others' emotions for me. When a friend tells me she or he loves me or when I feel the love of an animal, I want to be able to take that in, to accept it, to feel warmed by it. Likewise, when I love a friend or an animal, I tell her or him so. I can feel that in my body as well, my heart feels open and my belly is all warm and relaxed. Or, to give another example, if I feel moved by a remark someone makes, I say it and thank the person.

In group, Bob so often pointed out that others do not make our emotions. We do. It is important to keep in mind that the other person does not move me, does not make me feel an emotion or think a certain thought. I make that myself. Of course, it works the same way with negative emotions, anger for example: the other person does not make me angry – I make that myself. Why? What is happening inside of me and my body because of what the other said or did? How do I want to deal with upcoming thoughts and emotions? It oftentimes requires taking a deep, hard and painful look at myself. Perhaps I felt angry because the other spoke the truth? Or I felt so moved because that something (love, excitement, compassion, to name a few emotions) is missing in my life? There is a nice expression in German "how you shout into the forest, that is how it will come back" meaning that what I put out there is likely to come back to me the same way. That saying applies both to me, to how I treat myself as well as to the external, to others around me. I observe how I talk with myself, how I treat myself – am I even fair to myself? Would I treat a loved one this way? Would I treat animals and nature that way? They are all fellow beings on this planet earth with us, we all deserve to be treated with loving kindness.

"As the Buddha said, hard as it may be to embrace, 'you can

look the whole world over and never find anyone more deserving of love than yourself'," Stephen Levine writes in *Unattended Sorrow*[1].

On The Beach

Nature always calms me down and puts things into perspective. I drove to the ocean today. The closest, large beach is about an hour away from my house.

I have made myself comfortable out here, with an umbrella, blanket, chair, coffee and water, some snacks, and of course, with my journal. I only see two other beach parties. They are far away. It is so nice here. I can already feel my serenity return. Every time I am in untouched nature or when I commune intensely with my cats, I feel this way. All of nature is so immensely awesome and beautiful.

The little wading birds are not disturbed by my presence. They hurry back and forth at the seam of the water, picking here and there. I enjoy listening to the water making contact with the shoreline. I hear so many different sounds: there is the usual crashing of the waves against the shore, from the left I hear a brief gurgling, some unorganized splashing is going on as well; it sounds almost careful even. Now! That was a more serious wave coming in!

On the gulf here in Florida, high and low tide are usually only about one or two feet difference, so it is hard to tell where the water is at the moment. There! A small flock of the little wading birds sweeps in. There comes a bigger bird – off they fly. Two pelicans are skimming over the water – I am always in awe how they do that. It seems there is not even a foot of air between them and the surface of the ocean! A little whitish seagull dive-bombs – and catches a fish! I can see it glimmering in the sun.

Prime real estate is in high demand on the waterfront. The white sideway-crabs dig their houses real fast, the sand is flying around. They really do move sideways – it takes a moment to actually realize that. It is challenging to spot them, the crabs are so white, and they blend in real well with the Florida beach sand-color. I hope I did not come too close to their burrow-houses when I sat down on my blanket and spread my things around. I sure do not want to disturb them or any other wildlife out here.

It is always different at the beach, from moment to moment and from day to day. All is in motion. The clouds, the waves, the sand, the animals; it is the circle of life.

Now it is the grief I will move through. It is another circle of life, another process! If I try to be perfect – which in itself is not possible - after all, what is 'perfect', who determines that? - I cannot participate in the circle of life that is always moving. And I cannot be positive and enjoy life either.

Oh, I saw a fish jump! The ocean is still warm, about seventy-nine degrees Fahrenheit; it feels like being in a bathtub. I swam in the water earlier.

It is so great here at the beach. So peaceful. Now there are only two other people here, far away. I can let my soul dangle – *seele baumeln lassen*. That is a German expression that means to relax and be at peace. It always, always comes back to being in the moment. "We keep so much of ourselves at a 'safe distance' from the rest of our life that seldom do we directly experience the moment;" Stephen Levine writes in *Unattended Sorrow*[2]. Right now: I actually am all that. Here at the beach, I am in the moment.

I can feel it, sense it, ever more in myself: the hunger for life, the love for everything and everybody. It is right here. I oftentimes not only prohibit myself from being myself, from letting myself BE, I also resist being present, since I sometimes cannot see or grasp what that means.

Dolphins! I see them jumping! They are far out there. And just like that, I am in the moment again.

I love seeing the freckles of sunlight on the waves. The water here is a bit muddy; it appears brown and copper, so the sun shimmers golden on the surface. The glittering reminds me of all the thoughts that come up. They light up, I note them, they go, and another one comes. The waves do make it to the beach eventually – and the sun freckles are still there, there are evermore. Two Dolphins! Right at the shore! It looks like they are just two, three yards away.

On the drive home I notice, once again: being at the beach, in nature, grounds me. I do trust myself more. That is good.

Moving On

It is a crisp, sunny morning, pleasant seventy-two degrees Fahrenheit. It feels cool after the hot summer. The sun is out and looks fresh. The hummingbirds are here – it is so great to see them again. I marvel at their beauty and their abilities. Water drips off the lawn furniture from the night's rain. Amber licked off the water on the table, now she sits on a chair outside, soaking up the sun. Blackie is inside with me, Artus washes himself on the floor. Now head washing is going on – Artus jumped up on the chaise. He and Blackie give each other head-baths!

Yesterday I looked through old photographs of Carmelita. I will put together a collage about her. I found so many photos of her looking like a regal, content, healthy tortoiseshell-colored cat-queen! I called her Carmelita Chocolate Paw; one front paw had that rich brown color. In the photographs she almost looked like a different cat with a shiny coat, healthy weight, self-conscious, self-possessed and strong, with a confident expression in her eyes and body, my Carmelita-Cat! Seeing those photos, however, made me realize, I have given her the gift to really come into her own, to live a good life and to enjoy herself. I am so glad I discovered that. I found a photo of her where she carried a ball in her mouth – she loved to play with balls. She was so thrilled to have caught it that she paraded around with the ball in her mouth, showing her prize, proudly meowing around it! Which of course sounded funny, quite muffled in fact.

Many other memories of her come to mind: Carmelita rolled around in the grass when I sat outside. She followed me around. She wanted catnip after a meal. It aids with digestion. She enjoyed playing with tassels and the red laser light. I saw her playing with her tail. Adult cats only do this when they are being silly and feeling comfortable.

Because of her back injury, Carmelita always was a bit unsteady on her feet and really never could jump very skillfully. Occasionally she did want to get down from something or jump from a chair to the sofa which was always a major production. She measured the jump carefully, took real good aim – and then made a huge lunge for just a little ways. If I happened to observe that, I always made a big show of praising her – she was so very proud of herself.

Once I saw she and Artus engage in a ballgame together: sitting across from each other they pushed the white ball back and forth between them. Wow! That was a special moment. I did not realize it: I am and was so proud of her; of all my cats, really. Carmelita accomplished so much in those seven years she was with us!

How come I have forgotten so much about Carmelita's life? How she used to be, how healthy and playful and all? What does it mean 'to go in?' Into the grief, that is? Does it have to do with being in the moment all the time? Or is it a reminder of how life goes on, how it is constantly changing, that nothing ever stays the same?

That last line reminds of one of the songs we sing in Velma's singing circle I attend: "*I come from Women.*" Amy Carol Webb[3] just sums it up so nicely. The singing circle has enriched me in so many ways; all the nice women I have met there, or Velma with her admirable gift of being able to just pluck a desired note out of the sky, or to be able to play so many different instruments, some even simultaneously, or her voice that frequently gives me goose bumps when I listen to her sing. It is also the way Velma leads the circle; her uniqueness, her love and warmth and humor that spills over to all of us. And we give it back to her and to each other. It is healing and safe to be in there.

I have not heard music yet. Carmelita was deaf at the end, perhaps that's why. Cats are so sensitive to music, anyway. Perhaps it is just that: letting life be, with me in it, not resist writing or doing other creative projects. All this is very much in the moment, no wonder I feel resistance. Another thing is to be still, to be patient, to just be. Not bustling around with some activity that is not needed, that just fills time.

I hesitate. I do not want to move on. I am not done here, not done with this part of my grief. I still feel partially numb, as if I am not yet able to access it all inside of me. In Rita Reynolds' book *Blessing the Bridge*[4] I find comfort: "…Choosing to wade right in and gather that warm body and soul close to me and comfort him or her in the dying process usually takes tremendous courage. What makes this easier is my belief that my actions, thoughts, and prayers reverberate into all the depths of life. They reach beyond the five senses of our physical reality and touch every aspect of body, mind, heart and soul." Yes, I believe that as well, I can breathe into that.

Today I noticed that for the first time since Carmelita's death, Artus sat in the bed which is in front of Carmelita's hut. The hut is still here.

It seems to me, Artus wants to move on. I myself am not yet there. I am still quiet and contemplative.

Stephen Levine[5] writes that when we "open our hearts to our pain and to our hopelessness, we find that we are never truly helpless." He goes on to write that when we go into the pain instead of stuffing it away or ignoring it or moving away from it, then "something deeper arises: a mercy that leads toward the heart." It leads to ourselves, to self-mercy: "In order to open our hearts to our pain, we must be willing to experience it wholeheartedly."

Rita and Stephen both said the more we let ourselves experience life with all its pain and grief and heartbreak, the more we are able to love, to give love. I sense that, I feel that, I tell Amber and the two males every day several times how much I love them.

A hummingbird woman sits on one of the tiny light bulbs of the light garland outside. I have a big smile on my face. Hummingbirds are magical birds.

And Amber purrs so much.

A happy and healthy Carmelita Cat

Carmelita and Artus in the grass

Carmelita playing with a ball

Carmelita with her friend Blackie

Chapter 4

Amber

The Bump on Amber's Head

Sometime in Mid-August of 2010 I noticed a bump on Amber's forehead, right above her left eye. A bite, I thought. A bruise, a friend suggested; or a cyst, another friend said. The bump did not get any smaller over the next couple of days. If anything, it looked bigger, about the size of a Ping-Pong-ball.

So we went to the doctor. He took a biopsy right away; "It looks like cancer," he said, "I am sorry." I had tears in my eyes: my lovely, opinionated, red-haired Amber Lionqueen. I feel very sad. It will take a few days for the results to come in.

The next morning, Amber has fully recovered from her sedation. She is wandering around the yard; I just saw her passing by. I will think thoroughly about each and every step, about each and every visit to the veterinarian. My intention is always to help her get better, and not to inflict an additional wound or another trauma on her for no reason.

Amber's biopsy wound was at least a centimeter long (approx. 3/8 inch). The doctor had closed it with just two stitches – and the next day the wound had opened up again! Since it was right on her forehead, the open wound was in a very vulnerable position when she moved around the yard through the bushes and undergrowth. I could not see myself following her, pressing a cloth on her head to stop the bleeding.

Of course, these things usually happen on weekends. I noticed the gaping wound about five minutes after all the veterinary hospitals had closed on Saturday.

Off we went to the emergency clinic. The doctor there suggested using staples which would only take a few minutes – without sedation. They did that, but Amber hurt a lot and was very stressed out after the procedure. Poor cat. I also had not realized that those surgical staples do look like paper staples! Now she had four or five silver colored metal clamps sticking up on her forehead - yikes! I told her it is the new fashion these days, very trendy! I do not think she wanted to be fashionable, though.

Well, at least those trendy clamps did the job; the wound healed nicely. The doctor had given me an antibiotic since the wound was open and dirt could have gotten in. I did give her that for a few days. Amber was visibly in pain at the emergency clinic, so I asked about a pain medication – and then I ended up not treating her with that.

On the internet I saw that this medication has a lot of side effects. Treating pain in cats is difficult – all the available medications have side effects. Even Aspirin is toxic to cats. Lots of love helps though.

The next day Amber was okay again, she did get used to the staples – as much as one can get used to metal in one's forehead!

I did decide, however, that it was too risky to let her out at night. Too easily she could get caught in something, even if she just hooked a claw under a staple. She had already scratched some out, I noticed. Since I have a cat door – everybody had to stay inside. Artus was okay with that – "for now," he said. Amber was still a bit exhausted; she did check the cat door a few times and then settled down somewhere.

Blackie, however, would have none of it, "What's going on here?" he wanted to know. "This is not okay! I need to be out!

There might be boogie people in the house! Unbelievable! OUT! I want O-U-T!!!!" All his shouting was underlined by him running from the cat door to the French door and back.

I explained the situation to him, about his girlfriend and the staples and everything. "But," he pointed out, "what is it with those boogie people inside?" Well, he was right; there were friends here during those days. I told him he had to tough it out this time. After all, he could always hide in my office.

If I settled down – he did give in to his fate, and we all spent quiet nights with him and Amber stretched out on my bed. Artus slept in the colorful chair beside it.

Of course, in the mornings, I awakened by Blackie's insistent "OUT! Get UP!" – meowing. That was okay, they all could go outside during the day when I could monitor Amber.

Those days were long days. The biopsy was on a Friday, the results wouldn't be back until Wednesday. I did not want to think about it. I could tell Amber had slowed down. The staples in her head reminded me of it every time I looked at her. But – I did not want to go there.

Until Wednesday.

On Wednesday afternoon, the doctor called. "I am sorry," Dr. G said, "It's a sarcoma. They couldn't make out the kind, but it's likely to be a fibrous sarcoma. It's fast growing. I am sorry," he said once more. He had suspected that right away when he made the biopsy. To have it confirmed just made it sink in more.

We discussed some options – there really aren't any. We decided to let Amber be for now. At a later date we could think about giving her Prednisone, the doctor said. Surgery was impossible because of the location, right above her eye. The cancer could possibly affect her brain at some point as well. Dr. G thought her decline would go fast, more like weeks rather than months, he said.

The next day we went in to have the staples removed. Those clamps started to get itchy, I could tell. Amber was trying to scratch at them – and she would hook her claws under one – dangerous, that.

Dr. G, my regular doctor, was not in; the new veterinarian there needed some time to get the remaining three staples out. One was somehow twisted and stuck in Amber's head. I felt so sorry for my furry cat woman. Finally, all three clamps were out and we went home.

It took Amber two days to recover from that experience. I let the cats out again at night, and she just stayed out all the time, lying in that little flower-bed with the pine straw and the amaryllis.

Eventually, Amber enjoyed life again: snuggling up to Blackie, her friend. They have a daily wash-in! One evening I saw her pummeling the catnip banana – Amber loves catnip.

During my lunch the other day she was on the dining room table for a love-in with me: she lies on the paper I am reading. She throws herself around and purrs up a storm. Of course, I am supposed to pet her all over – I happily oblige. OH! That feels good, she says. Love always feels good – to both of us.

The bump on her head is very visible. She has scratched up the scab from the biopsy wound; it is a little bloody still. But Amber eats and grooms herself. She is alert and interested. She is fine, even if she has slowed down a tad. She sleeps more and her sleep is deeper, I observe. It seems she is more exhausted as well. Today she played, running across the lawn, balancing on a border around a flower bed. My heart went out to her and I thanked her for showing me her joy in life.

A few days ago I came home at dusk; the sun had just gone down. As I drove up to my house, two live sentries were sitting out front – one was orange, the other black and fluffy! Amber and Blackie had positioned themselves in the front yard sitting in the exact same positions with ears alert at my approaching car, waiting for me to come home – dinner was late already!

I hurried in to feed them all.

Pockets in Time

Today looks like another glorious October day here. The heavy, moist Florida summer seems to be over; there is crispness in the air now. The mornings are cool; it is below seventy degrees. A female hummingbird still uses the feeder – I will refill it later today. It has been six weeks since we lost Carmelita.

These little oasis of being in the moment, of having peace, 'a pocket in time' - this is what I live for these days; it keeps me sane. I am here for my cats. I want to be here for Amber, go with her – hand-in-paw – so to speak, until the end.

We are all, the four of us, on the chaises with the doors to the deck open. I got the wool-blanket out today – they all LOVE to sit on it and make biscuits, making a kneading motion with their forepaws. This is a comforting behavior left over from kitten hood: kittens use their front paws to massage their mother's nipples to stimulate the milk flow.

Artus is on my lap, Blackie to the left, Amber to my right. I could sit like this all day – and I will.

Yesterday Amber was gone all day. Finally, around ten thirty at night I found her in a flowerbed. She did not even want to come in. Something had happened: her eye with the tumor above was bloody and she was disoriented. I carried her inside and put her down in front of her food dish. She ate only a bite or two. Later I started hand-feeding Amber on the chaise and then she finally ate on her own with an appetite.

What can I do for her? I asked her that too. It breaks my heart to see her like this. I feel like there should be other things I do not know about, something I did not check out! What did I forget? What did I neglect to do? I feel so helpless. Am I supposed to learn something to help her? I rattle myself with what else I can do for her, what I could have done for her. The only thought that comes into my head is "I'm fine. Don't fuss."

I have scheduled a phone appointment with Sharon, an animal communicator in California. Rita Reynolds recommends her in her book *Blessing the Bridge*[1]. The appointment seems to be a long time away, next Saturday.

I have started reading poems to the cats. I think Amber likes the poetry of Rainer Maria Rilke. I read it in German – she gets up and kneads with her front paws on the blanket, she 'makes biscuits' and purrs and purrs. I always talk German to the cats, so perhaps the special melody of poetry appeals to her. Today I read ***Der Schutzengel***[2]

"Du bist der Vogel, dessen Fluegel kamen,
wenn ich erwachte in der Nacht und rief.
Nur mit den Armen rief ich, denn dein Namen
ist wie ein Abgrund, tausend Naechte tief.
Du bist der Schatten, drin ich still entschlief,
und jeden Traum ersinnt in mir dein Samen,-
du bist das Bild, ich aber bin der Rahmen,
der dich ergaenzt in glaenzendem Relief.
Wie nenn ich dich? Sieh, meine Lippen lahmen.
Du bist der Anfang, der sich gross ergiesst,

ich bin das langsame und bange Amen,
das deine Schoenheit scheu beschliesst.
Du hast mich oft aus dunklem Ruhn gerissen,
wenn mir das Schlafen wie ein Grab erschien
und wie Verlorengehn und Entfliehn, -
da hobst du mich aus Herzensfinsternissen
und wolltest mich auf allen Tuermen hissen
wie Scharlachfahnen und wie Draperien.
Du: der von Wundern redet wie vom Wissen
und von den Menschen wie von Melodien
und von den Rosen: von Ereignissen,
die flammend sich in deinem Blick vollziehn,-
du Seliger, wann nennst du einmal Ihn,
aus dessen siebentem und letztem Tage
noch immer Glanz auf deinem Fluegelschlage
verloren liegt…
Befiehlst du, dass ich frage?"

The Guardian Angel

English translation on Tribe.net (edited by the author)
You are the bird whose wings came
When I wakened in the night and called.
Only with my arms I called, because your name
Is like a chasm, a thousand nights deep.
You are the shadows in which I quietly slept,
And your seed devised in me each dream, -
You are the image, but I am the frame
That makes you stand in glittering relief.
What shall I call you? Look, my lips are lame.
You are the beginning that gushes forth,
I am the slow and fearful Amen
That timidly concludes your beauty.
You have often snatched me out of dark rest

When sleep seemed like a grave to me
And like getting lost and fleeing, –
Then you raised me out of heart-darknesses
And tried to hoist me onto all towers
Like scarlet flags and bunting.
You: who talk of miracles as of common knowledge
And of humans as of melodies
And of roses: of events
That in your eyes blazingly take place, –
You blessed one, when will you at last name him
From whose seventh and last day
Still a brilliance can be found
On the beating of your wings…
Do I need to ask?

I wish I could just stroke and pet the bump on Amber's head away. It is so very hard to witness her decline, and not to be able to do more for her. I talk with her and explain things. I ask if I could do something, anything else for her. Part of me already lets her go a bit. No, it is not like giving up, it's more like letting life be - whatever is supposed to happen. I do observe her closely, having just lost Carmelita I try to protect myself from dealing with another loss. My little lion queen; just writing this makes me tear up.

This morning, Amber and Blackie were on the bed with me again – we had a big 'love-in;' lots of petting and stroking and purring and cuddling. The cancer grows as I write. It covers the entire left side of her head now. It has started to look grotesque, quite deformed. There is some swelling and a red rim around the eye – I cannot determine whether there is discharge from the eye or Amber scratches at it. It is bothering her, of course. She rubs it often, and Blackie washes her face there as well. It surely must affect her vision now.

Amber does not seem to be in any pain. She might feel some discomfort perhaps. She is on homeopathic remedies and I give her Bach Flower Essences. I gently wipe her eye with luke-warm water to get the discharge off. She let me do it this morning, which is good. I will start the Prednisone now as well.

Our mornings together, our pockets of time, have become even more precious to me – it is quality time I spend with her and Artus and Blackie. It is bonding time. Love time. Mindful time. It is cherished time together.

I tell her and the two males all the time that I have a limitless supply of love for them – as much as they want and more.

On my cat calendar it says today:

"Er war alles fuer mich" = "He was everything for me"

They are. All of them.

A Poem for Amber

My lion queen is not doing so well – she was not on my bed at night and she hides under the chaises. The cat door remains closed at night. It is safer.

My heart goes out to my little lion queen. I cannot even grasp how it will be with her gone! She is such a steadfast companion and good friend to me and Artus and Blackie. How will life be without her? I have learned, am still learning, so much from her.

Her independence! She speaks her mind, she speaks her truth! And – if it did not happen the way she wanted it – she let me know! She goes for what she wants, what she believes in. A lion queen she is! Her body might be the size of a housecat, but her personality sure fits a lioness!

She is a great mother – when I got her from the shelter ten years ago she had two kittens. Thin and sick herself, she still provided them with the best care. She is a great huntress. And – above all – she is my lion queen-catfriend: Amberli, my sweet little brave lioness Amber. She is ever sweeter now, wants to be with me and purrs up a storm. It is like she needs me to hold her, be with her and she rests with me. I feel honored that I can give her that.

She ate a few bites; I did not see her drink. Now she is in the guestroom, behind the futon. That seems to be a good hiding place – Carmelita was in there a lot as well. Amber sits in there and purrs. I rack my brain; what else I could do for her. I desperately try to hang on – to what!?

I have such pain in my heart- and throat-chakras; it is so very hard to lose loved ones.

And – once again – I have a difficult time staying in the moment to just be - compassionate and loving to not only the cats (and my human friends) but also, most important, to myself. I want to go into the grief and not resist it.

I wrote a little poem for Amber, that helped with the grief process:

Amber, meine kleine loewenkatze, (Amber, my little lioncat)
With the spirit of a lioness
In the body of a cat.
Dein fell glaenzt rot-golden in der sonne, (your coat shimmers red-golden in the sun)
You walk this earth
With elegance and beauty.
Du weisst, was Du willst, (you know what you want)

You always speak your truth.
Du liebst Deine unabhaengigkeit, (you love your independence)
You would not have it any other way.
Es gibt nicht genuegend worte (there are not enough words)
To say how much I love you,
Admire you and learn from you.
Ich bin fuer Dich da, (I am here for you)
All the way to the end of your life.
I cherish you. I love you.
Forever and always.
Fuer immer und ewig.
Ich danke Dir. Ich liebe Dich. (I thank you. I love you)
Du bist alles fuer mich. (you are everything for me)
Und eines tages sehen wir uns wieder, (and one day we will see each other again)
At "the other place."

The Angel of Tears

I had a long phone conversation yesterday with Sharon, the animal communicator.

She said that Amber feels really sad she has to leave so shortly after Carmelita. And Amber is sad for me because I am crying so much for her. But she thinks it will be good for me to have my heart broken open more, so that I can finally process my old grief. Amber told Sharon she saw the angel of tears, who collects the tears of people who cry for their beloved animals. The unused tears then turn into diamonds for all the animals for whom nobody cries and who die alone. What a lovely thought – I like that, it is comforting.

Sharon said the cats like it that I treat them as friends and let them live their lives; they are of a different species, but with their own personalities and things to do and all that. I know them quite well from my point of view. How else would I treat them if not with my own compassion and love, with human ideas and human ways? Sure, we might know a few things about cat behavior and proper cat-etiquette but is it not a mere glimpse of their world? What do we really know about cats – or any other animal, really? How do cats tick? What is important in their world - aside from the basics we all need, like love and food and shelter? What do cats like? What do they love, what is of value to them?

We – our generation at least – will not know all the answers.

I see ever more how vital, how important it is to treat myself with love and respect and compassion and loving kindness. As Stephen Levine[3] writes "Hold your heart softly."

If I do not do that for myself, if I do not start with me, how can I expect another person to treat me well? In our society, care for others is given more praise than people who do their own thing, live their lives. Sadly so, I would say. This is not about being mean to others, or disrespectful or unloving – it means quite the opposite. We all need to learn as much about ourselves as possible to be able to treat ourselves well and know what is good for us – and therefore for others. Stephen Levine[4] writes it well: "When we try to find out who we truly are instead of constantly attempting to be different, to, ironically, be better than the place within us where we are already perfect, we get ensnared in others' opinions of us. Meeting ourselves 'as is', practicing self-acceptance as a form of compassion and gratitude as a form of appreciation, we begin to find out who we are …." Cats know who they are. After all, they have been gods at one point.

I am still learning.

Amber is not well. Something in her brain is not right, it seems. Amber told Sharon that she cannot smell and taste very well anymore. Amber walked around the house quite disoriented and right over the plate with the dry food. I hand-fed Amber a few bites that she took and I gave her syringes of Pedialite and cat milk that she liked. And she already got her next dose of Prednisone. I made sure it is okay to increase the dosage.

Sharon said, "Amber does not remember much of when she was so out of it. She says, 'it seemed like a bad dream'." Amber does not hurt, her head feels stuffy and she is disoriented. I asked Sharon about the wandering around and she said she has seen that in her own animals as well. She calls it 'toning' - toning into the physical space, and not losing the connection. Amber said it looks worse for me than it feels to her. I think it might be a kind of walking-between-the-worlds-meditation: to still be grounded here on earth, in the physical realm, but also on the way out. I send out love – to Amber and Artus and Blackie and myself.

I read a prayer for Amber from Rita's book *Blessing the Bridge*[5]:

"May Amber receive the healing she needs. Help her to come into full awareness, with peace and ease, free of fear and suffering.

Help me find the inner strength, courage, and peace to do this work. Remind me that I am an instrument for healing that will flow through me.

May joy, understanding, and resolution be present. May Amber heal into the fullness of life, or into the light of Spirit. If death is the final healing, may this be achieved without pain. Let her passage into death and beyond be easy and comforting to her."

A Caramel Colored Day

And so it continues: Amber is just fine today! She was on my bed again, with Blackie. There was lots of purring going on. Amber woke me up by purring loudly – asking for food! That is something she always did like to do: waking me up in the morning by purring REAL LOUD, usually right by my ears! So cute. Or she would, still PURRING LOUDLY, make biscuits on my body.

Barbara comes to clean the house at nine in the morning, so we all get up early. The cats and I will be outside while Barbara is doing her cleaning magic. Right now, all three of them are on the chaises with me. Amber made a huge basket of biscuits on the wool-blanket, now she is curled up in there. Blackie sleeps on top of it, right beside his friend, and Artus is on my lap.

This is one instance where I love technology: We are all outside and I can use the internet via Wi-Fi. I have a cordless phone as well that works in the yard and the cell has reception around here anyway. It is so nice, sitting here with Artus on my lap, enjoying the quietness of the morning. The day is green and golden, almost caramel colored. Fall has arrived. Even my tea has this color.

Amber is washing herself; this is so nice to observe.

I learned a lot during the last days: I learned that I am fine right here at my house and in the yard with my cat-friends. They really are my friends, and I am learning to say that! They are important to me, and I feel connected to them. I feel comfortable admitting that - this is my truth.

Amber turned around - the other side gets washed.

My truth also lies in the quiet spaces in between when I can listen, feel inspired, and write. The last day or two I had rushed around too much – no quiet spaces left.

The cats are masters for stillness. They allow these quiet, open spaces to flourish. It seems they meditate a lot as well; perhaps they go into their parts of the collective unconscious. I believe purring brings them there. Our entire universe is stored in the collective unconscious – everything - since the beginning of our time. We are all connected.

I am learning to listen to my inside more, to go into my still-ness, to feel what I want or need, to determine what is impor-tant to me. I will make baby steps; it seems almost threatening to me to feel inside myself regarding large life-decisions.

I will start with small things, like a book a friend recom-mended – I looked at it and decided "No, not now, it does not fit in right now." I have come a long way that I feel comfortable to decline reading a book that I do not like but someone rec-ommended. Books have always been my friends. I found solace in books. As a child and teenager, I devoured stories of intact and caring families. Or I learned and rejoiced in stories where the characters faced obstacles only to have them lovingly resolved at the end. Books were a safe place to be – since my own life during my upbringing was so full of fear and unloving.

Once I got older I started reading not only more classical lit-erature but also a lot of psychological and self-help books.

One of the first books I found when I started therapy and became interested in psychology was *I'm Ok, You're Ok*[6]. I do not remember much about the book itself but I always remem-bered the title - back then I did not feel okay. I have always wanted to "be okay" – without really knowing what that is I was looking for or how to get there. I always knew, even when I was little, that my upbringing, the abuse, the pain and grief I felt and feel, the insecurities, the fear I experience, is not how

I was meant to live, or how life was meant to be. I was always looking for answers, to move on, make changes in me and my life. Finding that book marked another step on my journey to move beyond the grief, to find myself again, to live a life that is filled with joy and authenticity and most of all, love.

It is a quiet time right now. I do not bustle around so much. I stay off my feet – they are hurting. I will find out about the reason soon.

Humbleness comes up, paired with ever more gratefulness: Amber is still fine. I do take a tiny bit of credit for that I did not give up on her, that I did not make the final call to the doctor. Every day I give her – she gives herself – is a gift to herself and to us all. I am very delighted about it.

Amber is on the scratching post, making a "muff" with her front paws. What's that called in English? I am talking about the position where the cats fold their front legs together, so it looks like they have their paws in a "muff" to warm them, like women used in older times. It looks very cute, of course. My beloved lion queen.

Her coat is lush and plush; Amber wears her autumn colors well.

Herbst [7]

"Die Blaetter fallen, fallen wie von weit,
als welkten in den Himmeln ferne Gaerten;
sie fallen mit verneinender Gebaerde.
Und in den Naechten faellt die schwere Erde
aus allen Sternen in die Einsamkeit.
Wir alle fallen. Diese Hand da faellt.
Und sieh dir andre an: es ist in allen.
Und doch ist Einer, welcher dieses Fallen

unendlich sanft in seinen Haenden haelt."

Autumn

English translation on poemhunter.com (edited by the author)
The leaves are falling, falling as if from far up,
As if orchards were dying high in space.
Each leaf falls as if it were motioning "no".
And tonight the heavy earth is falling
Away from all the stars into loneliness.
We are all falling. This hand here is falling.
And look at others. It is in them all.
And yet there is someone, whose hands
Infinitely calm hold up all the falling.

Autumn Winds

Amber wandered around the house yesterday – she is 'toning' again. She does not drink or eat then – but when I hold up the dishes to her she takes the nourishment. It seems the cancer messed with her brain again, she has forgotten that she needs to drink or it just does not seem important to her anymore.

I think part of Amber just left; I saw a glimpse, an orange movement, pass by the chaises here in front of the French doors. Amber is still sleeping behind the futon.

The last three days I was busy running around for my stuff: my feet are hurting – plantar fasciitis, the doctor said. Other aches and pains are going on in my body as well. I feel there is so much grieving going on, it is a bit much. I had noticed some signs, some pains in my feet during the past years – I choose to ignore the pain.

Was it the same way with Amber? Had Amber just ignored the signs and the lingering pain? I would think all that shitty cancer must have started raging through her body prior to its visible outbreak. Amber had been a bit subdued for some time now. Otherwise she was okay. If there were other signs, I did not notice them.

We are all outside in the sun now! I coaxed Amber out from behind the futon, gave her some ham that she ate on her own! She drank a few sips of water and I gave her Pedialite and 1/8 of one of those pain pills, just in case. I do not know if she actually is in pain.

The autumn winds will whirl her away, my little lion queen. With her orange coat she blends in perfectly with the fall colors. This weather reminds me of Germany. Fall there is almost a violent affair: the cold comes in with heavy storms and tons of leaves fall from the trees. It is different here: from my chaise I see the azaleas blooming dark pink. My river beeches, which surround the azaleas, are decorating the grass with their leaves – they are all the color of Amber's coat.

I called Dr. G first thing this morning. He said I can double the dosage of the Prednisone, one tablet (5 mg) in the morning, and another one in the evening. Amber already got her dose this morning; I will give her another one at night, hoping this will help her. Cats tolerate Prednisone well, the doctor says. At least, that is one thing I can do for her. I believe this medication helps her, takes the edge off at least. I continue giving Amber the Bach flower essences and the homeopathic remedies.

Today I am tucked in here at the house, once again. Why did I run around so? In this case I urgently wanted to get it over with – the foot problem and finding shoes that I can comfortably wear. I want to make the pain go away. Fast. (So I can ignore it again.)

I am dreary, weary, wary – all of those, I think. Last night I was up several times, checking on Amber. I wish for her that she can leave smoothly, without struggle. I admit part of me hopes it will not be long now. I do not want her to suffer.

It is just the three of us on the chaise, Artus, Blackie and I. The river beeches in the yard lose their leaves like rainfall; even the noise is the same. I checked on Amber, she is sleeping, at last – deeply, it seems – behind the futon. My independent, free-spirited lion queen; I will live on for her in that free-spirit!

Another part of my family gets ripped out – with Amber leaving. I feel loving kindness and compassion for Amber, the two males and myself.

Zum Einschlafen zu sagen[8]

"Ich moechte jemanden einsingen,
bei jemandem sitzen und sein.
Ich moechte dich wiegen und kleinsingen
und begleiten schlafaus und schlafein.
Ich moechte der Einzige sein im Haus,
der wuesste: die Nacht war kalt.
Und moechte horchen herein und hinaus
in dich, in die Welt, in den Wald.
Die Uhren rufen sich schlagend an,
und man sieht der Zeit auf den Grund.
Und unten geht noch ein fremder Mann
und stoert einen fremden Hund.
Dahinter wird Stille. Ich habe gross
die Augen auf dich gelegt;
und sie halten dich sanft und lassen dich los,
wenn ein Ding sich im Dunkel bewegt."

To be said when going to sleep

English translation on poemhunter.com (edited by the author)
I would like to sing someone to sleep,
Have someone to sit by and be with.
I would like to cradle you and softly sing,
Be your companion while you sleep or wake.
I would like to be the only person
In the house who knew: the night was cold.
And would like to listen inside and out
To you, to the world, to the forest.
The clocks are striking, calling to each other,
And one can see right to the edge of time.
And below on the street a strange man walks
And disturbs a strange dog.
Beyond that there is silence.
My eyes rest upon your face wide open;
And they hold you gently, letting you go
When something in the dark begins to move.

The Lionqueen is fine today

Amber and I gave each other a gift yesterday – and each of us to ourselves as well.

I think she toned again, wandering around the house all night. I checked on her several times, each time rescuing her because she had gotten stuck someplace. In the morning I gave her the Prednisone, some water and baby food. I held her – she just sat – and then she struggled to get away.

I got my coffee and picked her up again, cradled her in my arm and just stroked her rhythmically. And this time she stayed and fell asleep.

I had calmed her down, got her to relax and sleep. She – as far as I recall – never slept on my lap before. Now Amber often leans into me when I pick her up. I can always tell when she is really asleep, not just dozing: cute little sighs surface, her legs twitch a bit and her feet do not flex anymore, they are just soft and relaxed. I noticed that her paws flex and the claws come out when she is not so relaxed – holding on to life, I suppose.

I can be afraid, resentful, tired, sad, or anything else – in the end it always comes back to: I am right here, where I want to be, loving my lion queen; giving Amber her dignity, wiping her face, watching over her, protecting her, keeping her safe. It is just something I do for a friend with whom I have shared ten years of my life, and whom I hold close and dear. It feels unreal almost: all is very quiet and revolves around my beloved furry friend Amber.

Today Amber is much better: she ate the dry food. I saw her drink water and she had a love- and wash-in with Blackie on the chaise. Now she is back underneath it – that seems to be the "I don't feel too good but kind-of-okay-to-be-in-the-main-room" –place for her to sleep in.

On Monday I talked with Sharon again – our conversations are always so enriching! We joked about all the technology that is available nowadays, and Sharon said, "Well, the cats are on space book and have cat net. They are all connected, and know what's going on." We laughed a lot about these thoughts, which are just true. We, all of us, are connected.

Sharon said that Amber is very aware that I have given her many more days – by not having her euthanized right away when she was not doing well. Many other people would have done that. I told Sharon I never got the signal from Amber, the sense that it is time to call the doctor.

Every time Amber starts her decline with wandering around the house again, 'toning' herself, her body, in the physical space, a part of her is leaving. This time I noticed her body was changing, her fur stuck out more (sick cats' coats always look like unwashed hair in people, sticking together and out, stringy, fatty); her body appeared more hunched over. Her whole appearance was kind of – well! – sicker looking. I nurse her, feed and water her, as long as she wants it, I will assist her.

I asked Sharon what it is that Amber wants – oftentimes she follows me around. I give Amber lots of attention and extra food but I think this is not always what she is looking for. Sharon said, "Amber is searching for peacefulness. She is restless. I imagine she feels the illness in her body. It is like a wave, surging through her." That makes sense to me – it often happens so sudden that Amber is off again. It sure makes me humble and grateful to see her doing so well for yet another day. By now, all my friends know that I am providing hospice care for my Amber-cat. A friend understood perfectly "Oh, you're on kind of a retreat." That is right. I am on a love-retreat.

Blackie and Amber are outside. He has already settled into the little flowerbed, while Amber is still in bathing mode. It seems to be especially enjoyable to wash and sunbathe at the same time. Amber sure is fine today. My cat guys are with me. All the time, at least one of them is close by. Just a moment ago Blackie was on my lap and Artus between my legs – they formed an upside-down T.

They know.

They leave Amber alone but they are aware of her not being okay. The left side of her head is twice as big as the right side now. The eye is a mere slit.

I am enjoying every minute with her. I feel raw and vulnerable and humble and grateful and full of love. Always and forever.

Poem from Rumi[9]

"Why does sorrow turn around the heart?
Do sad and cold hearts attract it?
For a loving heart is an immense sea,
With waves that make
The tallest domes whirl."

Amber Runs on Prayers and Prednisone

Amber is still doing just fine!

She is drinking, eating, purring, making biscuits, cuddling with her friend Blackie, sleeping on my bed, washing herself, washing Blackie, walking normally, jumping up on furniture, interacting . . . and sleeping a lot.

Just like always.

Almost.

I feel raw inside. Open.

It is a great gift to have my furry cat-friends with me and to share my life with Amber, Artus and Blackie. Through emails and my blog TheFairyDustPlace I have been in touch with my friends about her – and they all send continuously good wishes and prayers for her! Apparently, Amber 'runs' on prayers and prednisone these days! Many of my friends admire me; they say they see that I treat my cats very well, with compassion and all. They realize, they say, how hard it must be for me. Yes, I say, that it is. But this is what I want to give my beloved cats. It is not up to me to end their life when they are not ready. So far, I have not gotten a clear signal from Amber that she would want to leave, that it is time for euthanization.

I cherish our time together, day-by-day, hour-by-hour.

I have the doors open – it is not very nice weather today, just sixty degrees and cloudy. Amber went outside, looked around – and came back in. She did that several times. Now she is on the chaise with her friend Blackie. Lots of bathing was going on earlier. Blackie is such a sweet cat-guy. He comes to me often, butts his head and purrs. Just sweet.

Artus was on my lap all this morning. My lover cat, Artus.

It is such a joy to see Amber feeling so good; makes me feel so humble. Something inside of me is changing. I am becoming so much more open and aware. My belly feels like a gate has been opened in there. I feel so raw. I feel so much more intensely what is happening. I let myself feel that. For my Self and for the cats – I feel like I really am with them. I tune into them more, observe them, pay attention, love them more openly and I am more loving and observing towards myself as well. I pay attention and have compassion for myself.

These emotions go with what I wrote in my Morning Pages, of living free! Free of this constant fear and angst. I take life in more, I do not hide behind the fear, I am right here, dealing with whatever happens.

I am simply amazed and delighted by the bond I share with my cats, how in tune I have become to them – or we to each other. It is marvelous to observe and to experience their intellect and feline awareness, and their love and compassion.

I have heard people say or write that animals do not love and are not compassionate, that only we humans can feel that. I think that is nonsense. Cats (and other animals) might not have the word love for that emotion; after all, they do not live in such a word-world we do – but they have emotions and form bonds and friendships with each other and with us. They are intuitive as to what we humans feel, they sense that. Much faster and deeper than humans do!

Sometimes my cats re-act to an event, but I have seen them act compassionate or caring or loving on their own. It is Artus checking out distress-meows from Carmelita; Blackie comforting Amber, touching her, sitting side by side and all of them wanting to be with me, sitting with me, talking with me. I will never forget how, many years ago, Blackie showed his understanding and compassion on the day Sir Sam died. They did not get along at all. Sir Sam wanted to be a single cat; he did not like the other cats. On the day Sam died, he was sitting with me on a chaise outside, quite sick and pretty out of it. Blackie came over, hopped up on the chaise and snuggled up to the white cat, giving Sir Sam a quick lick behind the ears, all the while looking up at me to see whether I had noticed that. It was Blackie's way of telling me he knew Sam was going away – and of letting me know it was okay, they had all noticed, and wished Sam a good journey. I was so moved by that gesture. It was so caring and loving.

I realized today I have done all I can for Amber and I will continue to do so until the end. It is not my fault she dies. I cannot prevent death – it is part of life. I often go back in time these days, thinking about Mammi. I will make peace. I could not have prevented her death.

I feel so close to Amber: she is my friend, my little lion queen. Whatever happens, I will be okay and it is part of the circle of life: "…– the state of not perfect and it's okay; just trying to do the best I can with all my heart." Rita Reynolds[10] sums it up nicely. I absolutely do that.

Vorgefuehl [11]

"Ich bin wie eine Fahne von Fernen umgeben.

Ich ahne die Winde, die kommen, und muss sie leben,
waehrend die Dinge unten sich noch nicht ruehren:
die Tueren schliessen noch sanft, und in den Kaminen ist
Stille;
die Fenster zittern noch nicht, und der Staub ist noch
schwer.
Da weiss ich die Stuerme schon und bin erregt wie das
Meer.
Und breite mich aus und falle in mich hinein
Und werfe mich ab und bin ganz allein
In dem grossen Sturm."

Premonition

English Translation by Cliff Crego (edited by the author)
I am like a flag surrounded by vast, open space.
I sense the coming winds and must live through them,
While all things below do not yet move:
The doors still close quietly, and in the chimneys is silence;
The windows do not yet tremble, and the dust is still heavy
and dark.
I already know about the storms, and I am as restless as the
sea.
And I spread myself out and fall back upon myself,
And throw myself off into the air and am completely alone
In the immense storm.

May Amber have a peaceful Journey

My heart hurts. My lion queen is getting worse. Amber is weak,
she falls over a lot. She pants more; the bump on her head has
grown overnight. Earlier, I held her in my arm and when I had

to get up, I put her to the side – she just stayed there without moving.

"Listen, listen, listen to my heart's song.
Listen, listen, listen to my heart's song.
I will never forget you.
I will never forsake you."

I chant that poem for Amber many times. It is from Rita's book[12]. And I continue to read Amber the poem I wrote for her, and Rilke and Rumi-poems as well.

I already grieve for Amber – I walk through the house and see all the places where I stuffed pillows and cardboard in corners to prevent her from getting stuck - and I realize she will never be there again. Ever.

Sharon emailed to say Amber is peaceful and calm. Sharon said Amber knows the angels will come for her, and Carmelita will be there as well, when it is time. Amber does not want the doctor.

I am thinking that as well – Amber seems calm. On Sunday she walked around the house and then, she walked outside in the grass. In the house she followed the walls or the furniture – if there was an opening, she tried to squeeze through. I had to extract her several times because she got stuck. One leg went through but there was no room for the other foot. Outside she ambled around on the lawn, stumbling into holes, tripping over leaves. She scrambled into some bushes, wandered around in there – and could not get out, there were branches in her way.

She was toning herself again; her body – and part of her spirit – was still here in our realm. Other parts of her were already in the other place, in another dimension, where she, her soul, her essence, could just float through all the openings.

She let me hold her – I did that; as often as possible. She clung to my arm – for support? For grounding? All of that, I suppose. Last night, I had her in my bed beside me. Blackie was there, he washed her head. Then Amber struggled, she wanted to tone some more – I put her down and stayed with her – to help her if she got stuck somewhere. Then she slept on the bed with me some more; deeply, deeply, without moving. Another part of her, a large one, went away that night. I dozed off a bit, instantly alert when I felt her stirring.

Everything stands still, nothing at all matters – it is about Amber (and Artus and Blackie). Everything appears clearer, is outlined more. I am much more aware of what is going on. Hypersensitive.

I give her chicken baby food, water, Pedialite and Bach flower rescue drops and the homeopathic pain remedy and the Prednisone.

My heart hurts.

I watch over Amber, hold her, feed her, cry, extract her when she is stuck, clean up after her – and love her, love her, love her a lot.

It is pretty much all that is left to do. It breaks my heart. I wish my lion queen a peaceful journey. It is okay for her to go to 'the other place,' that is what she called it when she talked with Sharon about it. Of course, Amber is very aware of what is going on. Animals are so much better at accepting death than we humans are. I feel it is a sacred time to accompany a loved one into leaving. Time stops, it is the only thing that matters.

Prayer for Dying[13]

"Beloved Friend:
I, with you,
Resist nothing,

Move in peace,
Blessing this bridge.
Spirit we are:
Unified always,
Souls bonded
Through our love;
Now we are free.
Namaste"

I bear Witness

This morning, Amber could not walk anymore. She scrambled on the floor; she was making paddling motions with her legs. It was heartbreaking to see that. On the hardwood floor she could not get any traction, could not move forward. She did not want to drink water anymore, but I gave her the Prednisone and the pain medication.

I put her back on the carpet where she paddled around in circles; she hooked her claws into the carpet to get some traction to move forward. Then she came across the hardwood again. Kittens scramble like that as well – they paddle around, having no muscle tone yet in their legs. Sharon said death is just birth in reverse. Old or sick people – and animals – resort to behavior like babies, complete with diapers and having to be fed and all.

I am holding Amber in my arms today. I only put her down when I have to get up to go to the bathroom or get something to drink. All through those last days when I had Amber in my arm she held on to me, to my arm, for dear life. Sometimes she used my arm as leverage to steady herself, to not fall down, lose her balance, to just anchor herself, or to get sucked into the "in-between-space" again. She wanted to make certain she is still with me, still in the physical space. I am proud to wear the scars from her anchoring. I am sure Amber knows I am here and I am with her.

We went outside again – just a short while. I had the impression it was too much stimulation for her now – the birds, the leaves, the neighbors, cars, the wind. Back inside, sometime in the afternoon, her breathing became more labored, just like what I had experienced with Carmelita. Amber started walking then, moving her hind legs rhythmically. In a way it looked like she was making biscuits with them. Occasionally, she would stop and drop into a deep sleep.

In the evening, we had group here. Amber hung in my arms. She started walking with her front legs now, as well. I think during those two, three hours another part of Amber left. I felt that if she would not go this night, it would be time to call the doctor for her in the morning. It is so difficult. Both to be a witness to it and to leave one's body. Amber was leaving piece by piece. She walked all evening. Some of the group members said they could not even think about doing that, they would have had her euthanized days ago. That thought had often crossed my mind, but I never got a clear signal from Amber that she wanted the doctor to come. I propped her up in my arm, made sure she had air to breathe, and did not sink into a fold of my shirt or something.

After group I walked back to the chaises with her. Her body was just lolling about; she could not even scramble around on the floor anymore. I laid her on the chaise, put pillows and towels back in place, got something to drink for myself and I held her again. I realized all those hours it seemed she was walking through her life and toward the other place. Perhaps Amber saw loved ones and angels and wanted to walk toward them. Carmelita was waiting for Amber, I am sure. Sir Sam was there. And all the angels.

At one point Amber stopped her walking.

Artus and Blackie were right there with us on the chaise; they both came and touched her body. Both cats witnessed their cat-friend walk over the rainbow bridge. Amber's breathing had become raspier – I think at that point she had left her body and Artus and Blackie had felt that and said goodbye to her. They knew. It was healing for them to see Amber go slowly, rather than have the doctor come and she is suddenly gone.

I sang to her and read her all the poems she liked. I told Amber how much I loved her, how much I will miss her, and that it is okay to move on. At one point she cried out, it was like a release. I encouraged her to let go, to move on to the rainbow bridge and cross over. I told her it is okay. I recited the poem I made for her, I petted her. Her breathing was heavier then, sometimes it sounded like huge sighs. Then she started sputtering, several times – she threw up majorly at the end.

She had already left then. I held her for a few minutes longer and howled for her. Howls of release, of relief and grief.

Howls of saying goodbye to her, goodbye to my beautiful Amber Lionqueen. Howls to celebrate once more her life, to welcome her into the other place. Howls of grief for her and Carmelita and my mother and my other loved ones.

It is over.

Amber died in my arms last night at one twenty on this 23rd day of November 2010.

Heart Breaths

I am amazed at how physical this all is: my body feels weak and exhausted, my heart hurts, I am dizzy, my digestion is off, and I am not hungry at all. I am tired, and I struggle to breathe.

It is such a learning and growing process for me. I sit with the grief. I just let me be.

"The ancient practice of breathing into the energy center of the heart point can open a direct conduit to 'our true heart.' When we are breathing into and out of the heart, venting it to the surface, the heart breathes deeper. Our life reaches all the way into what makes it precious." Stephen Levine[14] writes that in his chapter *Heart Breath* – That is how I feel, I will breathe more deeply into the heart - love will come in and out. Am I resisting something here? It only helps for a second… It is yet too soon to fully go into releasing the grief. I pay attention to what comes up – there is a whole lot of unattended sorrow and missing love. I give myself patience and loving kindness.

Oftentimes when I sat with the lion queen, I knew it would be the last time Amber experienced rain on this earth – the full moon – the grass – the sun. It made me so sad and grateful as well: That I noticed it, that I celebrated it with her. I felt grateful for all the experiences I have here on this earth – especially with and in nature. It is the presence of every moment, to appreciate the beauty around us and take it all in and to accept it, to live in it and be of it.

Sharon and I had an enriching conversation again today. She confirmed that Amber had not been in pain, and that she did walk over to 'the other place.' Sharon thought that the entire illness and the transition of both cats to the other place put me through a transformation of my own and helped me along on my way. Amber is glad we did it this way together, she thinks it was initiatory for me, that I won't be so afraid anymore, that I can trust more, that I gained confidence in myself and that I can let go of my grief more.

"Something in us can transform such suffering into wisdom.

The process of turning pain into wisdom often looks like a sorting process. First we experience everything. Then one by one we let things go, the anger, the blame, the sense of injustice, and finally even the pain itself, until all we have left is a deeper sense of the value of life and a greater capacity to live it." Rita recommended *My Grandfather's Blessings*[15]. I will grow and gain wisdom, I know that.

As usual, Sharon sees cats all around me. Cats stand for feminine qualities, that is what I need to come into my own. Humans all need more awareness, more loving kindness toward each other and to all of nature.

I told Sharon I feel so forlorn – she said that is not surprising, it is grief. This time we talked more about me – the cats are fine, she said. "I can sense Amber as a lioness," Sharon said. But it is such a hole in my life here – I miss her so. Blackie said Amber will be coming back, she is so huge, like a lioness now, and she will bring lots of friends over to be around us.

It comforts me to think about my lion queen as a lioness – of course she is that! She and Carmelita both taught me so much. Amber was my independent female spirit the size of at least a lioness. Amber was so elegant and poised and beautiful. She had the most relaxed and the funniest sleeping positions. She woke me in the morning with huge purrs. She loved making biscuits, kneading the soft blankets, she had a huge presence, and she knew what she wanted and went for it. She loved to run after the laser light. She enjoyed cuddling up with Blackie and sharing baths with her fluffy friend.

Running away does not help, really. I did a lot of distractive stuff during the last few days. Then the grief comes at night. I have fear in my heart – exactly what Stephen Levine[16] says in his book, "… First we need to soften to our pain and send mercy into it, and then finally we can perhaps make peace with it." And we need to learn to open up and accept the pain with loving kindness.

I sang and danced for Amber yesterday. I lit candles, read all the poems for her, cried a lot. I asked Bob to dig the grave – it would have taken me way too long to do that. Bob was here for all of twenty minutes. It was quite matter of fact to bury Amber. That is okay. It fits her. Bob related an anecdote as well. A friend asked him what he was doing today and he answered: "Well, I had a dentist's appointment and now I am doing a cat burial and afterwards I will repair the roof on a friends' house!" His friend had laughed and said, "That is variability." *Ja*, rightly so. That is life.

I think it is a tremendous gift we can give each other and our pets to be there for them when they die. To open up and let it all wash through. There is always more love coming out at the end. "Love is never lost," as Stephen[17] so accurately observes.

Amber was and will be my lion queen forever.

The Aquarian Testament[18]

"When you come to me, know that we are both the Essence of God.
I will welcome you with honor, gratitude, and love.
And if you bring me anger, may I give you love;
If you bring fear, may I give you courage.
If you bring sorrow, may I give you joy;
If you bring uncertainty and doubt, may I give you peace.
And if you come willing to receive,
May I give you all that I am.
When you come to me,
I will see you and know you to be who you truly are,
Perfect in every way,

Always.
May all healing between us
Begin in the endless heart, yours, mine and that of all life,
Now and forever.
Namaste
(Sanskrit: I honor the place in you where we are one.)"

Young Amber

Amber's kitten

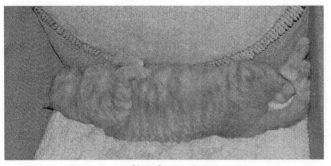

Amber in one of her funny sleeping positions

Chapter 5

Love Journey

The Orange Visitor

Ten days have passed since Amber left.

I sit on the chaise with my morning coffee, looking out across the deck. All of a sudden, an orange cathead pops up at the stairs leading from the deck down to the lawn!

My heart skips a few beats!

A second later I notice that the cathead belongs to a Siamese-type cat with beautiful, classic-tabby markings on her or his body.

The orange visitor ambles around on the deck, checks out the cat door, looks in on me and my cat guys through the French doors, walks around the other side of the deck, and disappears by jumping down at the side. A healthy looking fella, this cat has a good coat and appears to be well fed.

I had never seen this cat before, or – as yet – after. Was this Amber's doing? Sending someone over to say she is okay, and to look in on us – literally? That is a nice thought. My sweet Amber Lionqueen, I would not be surprised if she has had a paw in that cat's appearance.

I am pondering Amber's death and my own spirituality. What does it mean to me? Where am I in my life? What to do? How do I go on? I am deeply upset and disturbed by the death of my two beloved felines. Where did they go? What happens after death? How do I deal with all this? How do I want to live my life now? How do I finally make peace with my mother's death so many years ago?

Winter has arrived somewhat early in Florida this year – the month of December has barely started. It sure is cold here! Several blankets are piled on my comforter at night – topped by my two beloved fur-guys, Artus and Blackie. Blackie pretty much spends the entire night with me. He moves around with me, molds himself into the nooks and crannies my body creates. Artus usually joins us towards the morning – the house is colder then; I turn the heat off for the night. Artus chooses a place right beside me ---- and that's it then. He does not budge. Not even a millimeter. If I happen to turn around and dislodge him, he leaves; somewhat offended I can tell. He might come back later – or not. However, it is usually I who finds myself sandwiched between the two cats, oftentimes in a somewhat crunched-up position.

I feel very close to Artus and Blackie at the moment. I am not leaving the house much. I just want to be with them.

I am so very unsettled about the deaths – and life.

Amber is gone; my beloved lion queen.

And Carmelita went before her.

The Thing with Heaven

As a little girl when Mammi had died and for many years after, I steadfastly believed, that, yes, of course, I will see her and my grandparents and other loved ones again: in heaven, the heaven from the Christian religion belief system.

Back then I never thought much about it, I did not challenge these thoughts. During the last few years I noticed I do not believe in the church anymore; have not for a long time. After Mammi's death, with the stepmother our father married, all of a sudden we became Roman Catholics. I remember that as the child I was back then I felt confused about the transfer: is god interchangeable? Is there more than one god?

I had to attend lessons in the Roman Catholic faith to be prepared for the Holy Communion. I was taught then to believe in an old man with a beard and all that is associated with him: that this god watches over us and punishes us, and that we have to be good and follow the many rules associated with this religion. I had to go to confession and tell the priest about all the alleged sins I had committed. I recall I felt weirdly relieved afterward – a strange man forgave me that I had talked back to the stepmother – even though I knew it was unfair what she had done to me or my siblings. It was just like it was with Papa and the stepmother: he, Papa, was the law and he was always right and we had to obey him, no matter what. If I did not obey or dared to talk back to him he punished me – just like that god in church.

We had to go to church at least every Sunday, the god wanted that, we were told. Oh, the priests did talk about being nice to others; the god wanted that from his believers as well. Then how come Papa and stepmother fought all the way to and from church? And why were there so much anger and hate and negativity at my parents' house? Was this really what the old-man-with-the-beard-god and Jesus had taught? And why would they want to reside in such a cold big house when outside the world was so much more beautiful? I remember all these thoughts I had as a child, this religious church-thing just did not make much sense to me. Over the years, as I grew older, more serious and deeper doubts crept in. I started questioning the Roman Catholic values; I noticed they were not right for me.

The rules we were taught just reinforced the constant fear I felt during my upbringing – fear of my father, the stepmother, the god in our church, other relatives, school – without even knowing that I was afraid all the time. What I did know and what I hoped and wished for was a life of peace and harmony and joy. I knew – even as the child I was then – that a fearful life is not for me. As I grew older and moved out of my parents' house I started searching for a life without fear, for a life where I would be free of the grief and guilt I felt over Mammi's death.

At first I only rebelled against the church and religion and my parents' belief system. As I grew older and gained more knowledge I realized that I did not just want to be in opposition, I wanted my own truth and live my own life according to what is right for me. And that could not be a religion anymore; the triple set of negative experiences with my father and stepmother, the school and the Roman Catholic Church had installed in me a strong sense of wanting to be my own person. I just could not stand anybody telling me what to do or how to be anymore. I need to be free, free of fear, of grief, of anything that would hold me back on my path of inner knowledge, inner comfort.

In my twenties I set out – through therapy, groups, research, books, through the help of friends and mentors and the cats, with all of life really, to explore my innermost traumas and process my grief and let go of fear.

We all come into the world whole, as the person we are supposed to be. Then, through the years, through other people, parental - or lack thereof - influences and life's tragedies, like Mammi's death and the resulting trauma I experienced, we face challenges and get sidetracked. Life happens. We forget about our own magnificence and the unlimited supply of unconditional love we can give to ourselves.

I believe I can individuate again and become the person I was meant to be. This time being fully aware of what is going on inside my psyche, equipped with wisdom and knowledge and insights. It is, of course, a lifelong process, and requires commitment; a commitment to learn and to grow. I want my own truth, my own belief system. I am committed. Big time.

Spirituality

Bob arrived early for group on Monday, so I told him. I told him I was questioning all that heaven-theory. As a child I needed to believe that I would see Mammi again. It was a comforting thought, even a necessary thought for me in order to be able to survive the years of abuse following Mammi's death. I told Bob that now I was wondering whether I will see Amber, Carmelita, Mammi and all my other loved ones again. After all, no one really knows.

"You know, I have become so much more aware of myself, worked through lots of issues and I am so much more in the moment," I go on as Bob nods, "I feel I do connect so much more with people as well."

At that moment, other group members arrive.

Once everybody has settled down, one of the women wants to know how I am doing with Amber's death. I answer that I am having difficulties, I am still sad and do not feel well. The woman asks, "What is spirituality to you?" She looks at the others, "That's a group question, actually." I chuckle and say that Bob and I had just started talking about it: "Isn't it great how conversations and events and life so often fit together? I marvel at that." Then I get serious: "I am grappling with that topic big time right now. I think it's great you brought it up." I am quiet for a moment, and then repeat quickly what I had told Bob before, that I had always believed in some kind of heaven and that I would just see everybody again. "So, yeah, at this point, I don't know, really," I continue. "Spirituality is and always was, nature for me, the ocean, trees, the sun and moon, animals, all of nature, the connection with loved ones, of course, and always, always, the cats." I heave a deep breath before I continue: "I realize that even though it shook me to my core, I needed to experience a natural death. It was a bit much to see it twice just three months apart, of course, but it is challenging and helpful to me." I pause for a moment, look at everybody. "So, what is it for you," I give the question back to the woman who spoke earlier. "Yes, it is the connection with loved ones," she answers, "and with nature as well. My gardening gives me a great deal of that." I nod and say, "Yes, connection with others, I need that ever more. The concert with Velma on Sunday now that was extra special." I am quiet for a moment. No one interrupts the silence, it is clear I have not finished yet. "I think I really do reach out to people more," I finally say, "Just singing in the circle with all the other women, and then being part of the concert with Velma yesterday, that feels spiritual. When I said good-bye to Velma after the concert, I did tell her about these emotions." Here I choke up, "And that I so admire her. Yes, yes, I did choke up while telling her that," I smile. "The point here is that I don't think I would have done that in the past." Several group members nod their heads. They see that, they say.

While everybody in group gets a turn to talk about what spirituality means to them, I listen while I go and get several encyclopedias: "Tranquility," someone says, "Something greater than my Self," "Being in nature with my dogs" and always, they mention the connection with people. Since I occasionally look up something in my books, the group members are used to that. "We might as well get the definition of spirituality straight," I explain. Everybody is quiet as I close the books with a resounding thud: "Here, in the *Brockhaus Encyclopedia*[1]," I hold up volume 20 of all together 30 volumes of one of the best known encyclopedias in Germany, "there are about two pages about the subject of spirituality and such. Summarizing all that, I would say the original definition of spirit is really that it regards the human spirit as opposed to material, to physical things," I pause for a moment and continue, "In the *Oxford Dictionary*[2], the definition of spiritual is 'relating to the human spirit as opposed to physical things.' So it seems that over time spirituality became more associated with one's belief system or even with religion."

Bob speaks last: "Yes; for me, spirituality is to follow my own belief system. That is also in tune with Jungian teachings," he says. "So, if you say it is nature for you, you spend time in nature, you interact with your pets, or whatever. It also suggests that I update my belief system on a regular basis."

Once the group has finished and everybody has left, I hop on the internet to do more research about spirituality. I want to understand what exactly is meant by this word before I go into my own personal definition.

As is usual on the *World Wide Web* I have to wade through a lot of information before something useful pops up. Finally, I can sum it up:

Spirituality relates to something greater than us, something which gives meaning to our lives where we experience deep emotions and that fulfills our need to know, to understand and make sense of the world around us and the universe, to see the big picture – and its meaning for us as individuals – in all of life and death.

Spirituality is the narrative of our belief system that has to be valid and truthful for each of us, and it might change and expand during our lifetime, depending on our experiences, our life stories.

Spirituality can involve engaging in certain practices such as – for example - meditation, dance or chant. It can be religion, and/or the belief in a higher being. And/or it can be communing with nature and loved ones and being in the connective and creative flow of life.

Spirituality is anything that transcends us from our minds to our hearts where we feel and experience our deepest emotions.

Mothering

Just the other day I stepped into a nest of fire ants – my foot swelled up to be twice its size. I could not even walk. I told my dear friend Sally (who is very much a mother, she has three daughters), and she said, she is so sorry and it must be so painful and so on. And what did I do? Of course, I thanked her (it was on the phone, so she did not see my facial expression) but I felt irritated. No need to make such a fuss. I am tough. It will go away soon. No need to mention it. Sure, it really was not a big deal, but I noticed I always have a hard time receiving a friends' compassion for me. And I saw that yet it was because I cannot even mother myself. It is so alien to me, this mothering; I have no clue how to do that for myself.

There is a part of me, deep inside, that is so very delicate and small and vulnerable. It is my core, my pure, authentic Self. I want to protect this core while allowing it to finally flourish, like the first unfolding petal of a flower blossom, the first flutter of a butterfly leaving its cocoon – this part in me that is pure and small and - big.

After Mammi died, nobody was there to care for me and to

protect that inner core of myself. I was always alone since the age of six when Mammi died, I had no one who would be with me if I needed someone to hold my hand or comfort me. It was always just I, surviving. There was nobody left who 'saw' ME, who 'got me' and encouraged me to be who I am or wanted to be. I could not let anyone see ME lest I get hurt or abandoned again – and nobody wanted to hear about me or my grief anyway. Bearing witness to the natural deaths of my beloved felines has unearthed that fragile core in me. I allowed myself, for the first time that I remember, to go all the way inside and consciously face the grief, process all the deep emotions that came up and work through them with awareness and compassion and love for myself. In the years before I mostly stuffed my sadness away or just dealt with the grief on the surface, not with all the underlying emotions and thoughts. I stand in awe – and I am puzzled as to what and how to deal with all that comes up. I think this delicate part of my Self is something I have been looking for all my life. I am digging, carefully unearthing, like researchers do on an archaeological excavation, in my Self to unearth that fragile part of me as well as those negative complexes that keep me from really living, from seeing my Self!

Up to now I have always looked for answers in the external world – I am an extravert. However, extraverts tend to give power away to the external, putting other people or even things first. Extraverts also might not reflect back to themselves, "Is this what I really want? Is this important to me?" That I had to be so hyper-vigilant to my environs just added to that extraverted nature. But, no one can change me, my insides. No one can crawl inside my body or brain and tighten or loosen or replace the mechanics in there, like take out the grief, make fear go away - as tempting as that may sound, this ain't gonna happen. In the end, after all the reading and talking I am the one who changes. It is something I have to give myself, make for myself. I see that it is inside of me! I have to find out how to love myself, how to be okay with me, how to mother myself. I am the one who makes the transition into myself, into a more introverted nature and introspection.

Recently in group we talked about the archetypical role of mother and father. Bob explained that mothers give their children unconditional love, that it is okay and enough to just be. Mothers also teach about relationships, how to relate to others. Fathers do not do this unconditional-love-thing, they teach their children how to be in this world, issues like safety and security, functional relationships, how to put a roof over one's head.

I want to become a woman who is true to herself, who loves herself unconditionally; a woman who is a witch. Bob said that the original definition of this archetype means a woman who regards her own well-being above all else. In the last years I do like and love myself more and I feel more at home with myself. All the work I do has to do with that. It is all good to lead me on my way. In the singing circle we sang this week *Weave and Mend*"[3]. It is about gathering new insights and weaving new patterns and mending my grief. Fits right in.

Rain is dripping on the deck; the individual droplets make a little crater in the puddles, followed by the waves spiraling outwards. The drops, the grief, make a hole, a crater, inside me. I move on to heal it, to make the water that is my Self, smooth again. I begin by forgiving myself. Just writing that sentence brings tears to my eyes. Yes, I forgive myself for treating me badly, for beating myself up, for scolding me; after all, no one but me decides what I want to do, what feels good to me! I was told how to live by all the adults in my life and my shadow soaked it all up: show no emotions, be tough, dress appropriately, do not grieve, return all phone calls right away and so on. I forgive Mammi for dying and myself for wanting her back. I make peace with the shame I felt as a little girl and teenager for being different. I make peace with my guilt about not being able to protect my siblings more.

During my yearly visits to Germany, my siblings and I always spend some time together, just the three of us. This time I told them I wanted to move through my grief. And I told them about my guilt, that I was devastated that I could not protect them more – and both of them assured me that they had always felt safe with me! Wow – I cried, and felt so grateful!

I also visited Berlin: the town where my family had lived for so many years and where I was born. I thought perhaps I would pick up traces of Mammi, or that I might remember more, or get a feeling for where she came from. I did not know what to expect. I traveled across Berlin to the address where my father had lived. Mammi would have been at that apartment as well. As soon as I climbed out of the bus and crossed the street to look at the house I realized: Mammi is gone. It is over. I am free. Free of the past, free of her. I live my life. She is inside of me, in my DNA. And that is it. I do not owe her (or anybody else) anything. I do not have to feel guilty about living my life; I am allowed to live my life with joy.

We understand when we are ready for it. That is good to know. I am still scared to move through with all that knowledge, to accept myself, to acknowledge that I, indeed, am a strong woman. I still observe. I ask others and rely on others to tell me, to validate who I am – without realizing that I know this all for myself now!

I deserve to pursue my well-being, to be content and happy and well cared for by myself. That includes all of my life, small and big events, my body, my spirituality and my beliefs. And it means to acknowledge the dark side of myself as well; I talk with her, with the frightened and furious little girl part of me became after Mammi's death. I feel that it all belongs together. I need to pay attention to all the different aspects, not just to the intellectual side we address in group.

What an insight. I can be my own mother and enjoy my life. That is what mothering is: unconditional love. It was the one constant that stood out during the months of being with Carmelita and Amber: love. I am grateful to the cats. They show me how to do that. I could give them the love that I can also give to myself. Forever and always.

The Gift

Nobody wants to leave the house in the morning, even though I open the cat door right away. Instead, both cats are waiting for me to settle down on the chaise whereupon Artus jumps up and starts getting comfortable on my lap. Blackie also gets some cuddling done with me – he really wants to be hugged and cuddled - only by me, of course. "Everybody else is a boogie person," he says, "Yeah, yeah, I know, perhaps not – I keep looking and observing." He sure does that! I have noticed that recently he is not so panicked anymore by visitors – he stays around, remains visible. My friends all adore him. Blackie is such a gorgeous looking cat! He has an amazing set of whiskers, as well.

Of course, Artus, being TopCat, sits on my lap. Period. No discussion.

They do get along well, my two Furry Ones.

Eventually, the three of us settle in and we spend the next hours together on the chaises like this. It reminds me of one of those photo sequences, where a camera takes pictures at certain intervals – it would be funny to see how we move around here.

Friday is trash collection day in my neighborhood. In the evening I walked around the house, rounding up the various trash bins, paper- and plastic- and aluminum-recycling. Then I went outside, dumping it all into the big trash cans.

The cats were delighted to have me back after my absence during the afternoon – after all, dinner time was coming up – so they 'helped' with running back and forth with me, and inside and out with the small trash containers from the house. Blackie ran his usual commentary "Do you have to be so slow! Hurry up, will you, I am hungry! Oh, I like that noise (= paper rustling). Can I help? Wait, I'll come with you! What's for dinner? Yes, I like helping! Hey, Artus, oh, wow, look at this! Oh, I'll go over there! Aaartus! Come with me! Hey, it's nice here" and so on. Blackie is very vocal, what can I say! Finally, I rolled the bins to the curb – the cats stay away from me while I do that, it is noisy.

When I came back up the driveway, Artus and Blackie were running around – and I felt Amber's presence. She was right there with them, running with them, talking with them. The light had changed; there was a white and light-bluish luminance in the air. I did not actually see Amber, but I noticed her presence. I had tears in my eyes. What a gift my lion queen had given to me, that I could actually catch a glimpse of the other place, the other realm!

A few days before I had written an email to Rita Reynolds in which I shared my grief and my doubts about the cats' death. Here is her answer:

"I do hope you are finding some peace. I would bet Amber is still around you, watching out for you! Sometimes I will get a really strong thought about one of mine who has left, even years later, and I am sure that little soul has just checked in to see how I am doing. I really look forward to seeing them all again when it is my turn to cross the Rainbow Bridge! In the meantime, it's a good feeling to know love keeps us close despite our different 'worlds'."

Thank you, sweetheart-cat! Amber was right there with us.

Rebirth

It is November again, one year after Amber's death. I am staying home, watching over my cat-friends. In June of this year I invited Izzybelle Mango, a very pretty 10-week-old orange kitten, to live with us.

Once again, I come back home after two or three hours because of my cats. I watch the kitten grow and explore the world "adventure park house" as my dear friend Maria - who is very tuned in to animals - said. Everything is new to Izzy "oh wow, the pen falls down. Oh wow, there is a tassel. Oh boy, a leaf on the floor. Oh what's that noise?" I observe my kitten and I remember that with Amber during her remaining days I knew it would be the last time for her to sit on the chaise, to see the rain and be in the grass and feel the sun on her coat. Now it is a rebirth: for Izzybelle it will be the first time she feels the sun, hears the rain and sees a leaf. I live with her. I see her excitement over every new discovery – be it a drop of water, my pen moving over the paper, her tail twitching or a ball rolling on the floor.

It took me a while to get there. It was difficult for Artus and Blackie as well. Barbara from the Humane Society from where I adopted Izzybelle, said it best,

"I can't help think it is like Artus and Blackie's home is for them a very proper English Men's Club - quiet, serene, their personal "butler" (you), etc. Then this hyperactive kindergartner takes up residence - no wonder they are aghast!"

I laughed so much about it – that sentence just sums it up. I still giggle every time I think of it…

Blackie sits on his fluffy butt, one hind paw stretched out in front, washing himself thoroughly. Now he is kneading the blanket, his head goes with the rhythm. Then I see a black blob of fur on the chaise beside me; hair is sticking out all over the place. Hard to tell where is what. Blackie always decorates the furniture with generous dollops of fur.

Artus is working on an art project in my studio: I have some black foam boards leaning against the wall. He is scratching them and thereby turning them into three dimensional avant-garde art pieces. When he is not upstairs working, he sits on my lap, always. He purrs. He is supportive. He waits for me to sit down so he can be on my lap. Then he goes to sleep. Artus always looks out for me.

It is another pocket of time the cats and I have created for us. We all sit on the chaise, with the French doors open. It is the first real cool day; the first autumn winds give their concert in the river beeches. I hear birds singing. One hummingbird is still here, she uses the feeder. The winds have whirled leaves and red blossoms up on the deck. It is the circle of life once again. The autumn winds whirled my Amber Lionqueen away, now they welcome a new life, my orange Izzy-girl kitten, into the world!

It is healing. It is such joy to experience life through a kitten's awakening senses.

I am okay

It has rained today; a good thunderstorm with lots of thunder and a rich rain. I see some specks of sunlight filter through the trees now. Blackie is outside. He sat on the railing and then slipped down the back of a chair with his plume of a tail squished against the back. He contemplated for a moment "was this really what I wanted to do?" and then he turned on his side, thereby almost falling off the chair altogether. Now he is squeezed against the wall of the house – it is drier there.

The Izzygirl-kitten has grown into a sweet, beautiful Izzybelle-cat. She would like, if you please, to be called Izzybelle Queen now. "I feel like one," she says.

Blackie has become friends with her. There are love-ins and wash-ins and I think, the occasional play-in – Blackie has taken to playing a little with her. He had never learned that. Artus continues to be his usual loving self and remains top cat. And he is and always will be my lover cat.

Occasionally Artus gets bothered by the Izzybelle Queen and then he hisses and they crash through the house and ears get laid back and they get frozen in mid-air – that is always to see who will be the first one to move! And then, a little while after that, I see them walking side by side through the kitchen.

So, all is well in my cat world.

Looking back on the past year, I realize I have grown a lot. I have moved through my grief and I go through life with an open heart and awareness, with compassion and love for myself and everybody and everything around me. All events are sacred – it is all life and death, the eternal cycle of our universe. I am, each of us is, at the center of our own universe and we are part of everything. That is what spirituality means to me, the fabric of all of life, of the entire universe woven together. We are all god or the collective unconscious or Great Spirit or however we want to call the – ja, the universe where the tiniest particles, smaller than atoms even, are connected.

There is no judgment, no godlike entity, we are all interconnected and interdependent – and the guiding power is always love. It is the inner comfort, the mothering and the unconditional love I can give myself.

I understand that. It is the connection I feel with loved ones, be it Bob's group where I learned so much about myself; or my dear friend Kathy who so often says something that makes me pause before I realize that I just gained an important insight from her remark. Or it is singing in Velma's circle or it is through my longtime friends, like Sally, who is always there for me, sharing her wisdom. Or I am having a deep conversation with my dear friend Marlis who writes so well in her autobiography *From Now to Now*[4]: "I am living in a world of mirrors. Everything reflects back to me – what I am thinking, what I feel. I figured out over the years, that I always meet the right people at the right time, to show me, like a mirror, what I need to work on."

And it is always nature for me; I feel a bond when I hug a tree. I feel at peace when I sit with my cats. Just a few months ago, on a visit to California, I drove up to Castle Lake, a deep lake high up in the mountains. There was still snow around the lake and ice on the water. The sun made its sparkle patterns and everything glittered and I – sensed Mammi's presence there. I had not thought about her that day, but all of a sudden I felt she was there with me and inside me.

Yesterday I drove to the beach. It was sunny but cold and windy. Looking at the ocean calms me. It always does. Seeing the ocean, I think about endless possibilities. That is what life is all about. It is the circle of life; it is my life and my life story.

The other day at the singing circle, we sang *We are*[5] and one of the women, who had just returned from Australia, said the lyrics reminded her of the aborigines there who always talk about the dreamtime and that we all live in a dream story.

And for one long moment I had the feeling that all is well, that I am at peace with myself and the universe. I am always in my story. I make my paths now. I belong in my life, into my story that is colorful. I learn a lot and life is always new and continues on – in the spiral and the circle of life.

In our stories and in our dreams this and that happen, and we live always in our own stories that could also be a fictitious story told by somebody else. I tell my own story now, about Amber and Carmelita and Mammi, who all died and how I dealt with the grief and the pain. And I will tell other stories, about other lives and other people; and about other cats and other dreams that will be a true story for some and a dream story for others.

The trees dance in the wind. I feel myself in them, in their movement. They are wearing their new gorgeous green spring gowns. The sky dazzles in such a brilliant blue, it is impossible to paint. The earth is rebirthing herself. It is a rebirth in me as well. I step out into this world more and more, into my life, into my femininity. The easiness of being – a meaningful sentence I read somewhere and aspire to live up to. I trust life. It will run just fine without my holding up the day, which means feeling the urge to control every aspect of it. My original feminine nature is to trust life, to let life unfold and let myself be. I create life, with joy, in the moment. I am able to enjoy life fully and fully give back. I let the grief go. I feel safe. Looking back on my life so far I see that I have lived it well and handled all the trauma and challenges and experiences just fine. I am okay and I live the life that is truly me. I have my inner comfort and I trust life and I trust myself.

I believe in love. First and foremost. Forever and always. Love always lives on.

Blackie and Artus are good friends

The Izzygirl kitten at about 10 weeks

Izzybelle, the teenager

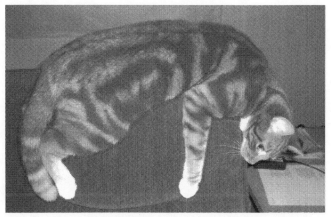

Izzybelle Queen she is now! She loves to sleep like that

Blackie, Izzybelle and Artus – they are friends now

Thoughts for the Journey

Writing this book has helped me move through the grief about Mammi's death. I can say today that I have really and truly processed my sadness. There will be other, new grief, more loved ones will die in my lifetime. But I have finally made peace with Mammi's death which I had set out to do when I started this book. Writing and witnessing my cats' deaths felt like a release. I could process and work through everything. I am very grateful for that experience. I have made peace with myself as well in that I allow myself to write, I let myself be. Even though it feels very personal to share my emotions and to get all my thoughts out on paper, which at times even hurts and involves pain, in the end I feel good that I have worked and processed this part of my life.

My life journey continues, of course, I have already started my second book, which will be about the relationship with my father.

I wholeheartedly agree with what Rita Reynolds and Stephen Levine write, that the more we go into our emotions, in this case the grief, and the more we let ourselves open up, the more we are able to love. That is what everything is all about.

We are all one and we are all in this life adventure together.

Be good to yourself and others and nature and enjoy life with love.

Bibliography

My Journey Begins

1) Barth, N. (May 2011). Das Haus meiner Mutter - My Mother's House. *Brigitte Woman*, 100-106.

2) Edelman, H. (1994). *Motherless Daughters*. New York, NY: Bantam Doubleday Dell Publishing Group, Inc. ISBN: 0-385-31438-8.

Love Lessons

1) Levine, S. (2005). *Unattended Sorrow*. Rodale Inc. / Holtzbrinck Publishers: ISBN-13 978-1-59486-381-3 ISBN-10 1-59486-381-4. Page 15

2) Levine, S. (2005). *Unattended Sorrow*. Rodale Inc. / Holtzbrinck Publishers: ISBN-13 978-1-59486-381-3 ISBN-10 1-59486-381-4. Page 14

3) Webb, A. C. (n.d.). *I come from Women*. Song. arranged by Velma Frye.

4) Reynolds, R. (2001). *Blessing the Bridge*. NewSagePress, Troutdale, OR: ISBN 0-939165-38-4. Page 71

5) Levine, S. (2005). *Unattended Sorrow*. Rodale Inc. / Holtzbrinck Publishers: ISBN-13 978-1-59486-381-3 ISBN-10 1-59486-381-4. Pages 18-20

Amber

1) Reynolds, R. (2001). *Blessing the Bridge*. NewSagePress, Troutdale, OR: ISBN 0-939165-38-4. Page 159

2) Rilke, R. M. (2001). *Spaetherbst in Venedig - Late Autumn in Venice*. Muenchen, Germany: Wilhelm Goldmann Verlag Muenchen ISBN 3-442-07737-0. Page 19

3) Levine, S. (2005). *Unattended Sorrow*. Rodale Inc. / Holtzbrinck Publishers: ISBN-13 978-1-59486-381-3 ISBN-10 1-59486-381-4. Page 46

4) Levine, S. (2005). *Unattended Sorrow*. Rodale Inc. / Holtzbrinck Publishers: ISBN-13 978-1-59486-381-3 ISBN-10 1-59486-381-4. Page 173

5) Reynolds, R. (2001). *Blessing the Bridge*. NewSagePress, Troutdale, OR: ISBN 0-939165-38-4. Page 72

6) Harris, T. A. (1975). *I'm Ok, You're Ok*. translation into German by Irmela Brender.

7) Rilke, R. M. (2001). *Spaetherbst in Venedig - Late Autumn in Venice*. Muenchen, Germany: Wilhelm Goldmann Verlag Muenchen ISBN 3-442-07737-0. Page 36

8) Rilke, R. M. (2001). *Spaetherbst in Venedig - Late Autumn in Venice*. Muenchen, Germany: Wilhelm Goldmann Verlag Muenchen ISBN 3-442-07737-0. Page 27

9) Kolin, M. M. (2009). *Rumi's Little Book of Love*. Charlottesville, VA: Hampton Roads Publishing Company, Inc. ISBN 978-0-9818771-2-9. Page 75

10) Reynolds, R. (2001). *Blessing the Bridge*. NewSagePress, Troutdale, OR: ISBN 0-939165-38-4. Page 121

11) Rilke, R. M. (2001). *Spaetherbst in Venedig - Late Autumn in Venice*. Muenchen, Germany: Wilhelm Goldmann Verlag Muenchen ISBN 3-442-07737-0. Page 38

12) Reynolds, R. (2001). *Blessing the Bridge*. NewSagePress, Troutdale, OR: ISBN 0-939165-38-4. Page 106

13) Reynolds, R. (2001). *Blessing the Bridge*. NewSagePress, Troutdale, OR: ISBN 0-939165-38-4. Page 75

14) Levine, S. (2005). *Unattended Sorrow*. Rodale Inc. / Holtzbrinck Publishers: ISBN-13 978-1-59486-381-3 ISBN-10 1-59486-381-4. Page 107

15) Remen, R. N. (2000). *My Grandfather's Blessings*. New York, NY: The Berkley Publishing Group ISBN 978-1-57322-856-5. Page 140

16) Levine, S. (2005). *Unattended Sorrow*. Rodale Inc. / Holtzbrinck Publishers: ISBN-13 978-1-59486-381-3 ISBN-10 1-59486-381-4. Page 119

17) Levine, S. (2005). *Unattended Sorrow*. Rodale Inc. / Holtzbrinck Publishers: ISBN-13 978-1-59486-381-3 ISBN-10 1-59486-381-4. Page 73

18) Reynolds, R. (2001). *Blessing the Bridge*. NewSagePress, Troutdale, OR: ISBN 0-939165-38-4. Page 73

Love Journey

1) Encyclopedia. (1993, 19th edition). *Brockhaus Enzyklopaedie*. Mannheim, Germany: F.A.Brockhaus GmbH, ISBN 3-7653-1100-6.

2) Dictionary. (2006, Fourth edition). *Oxford Dictionary of Current English*. New York, NY: Oxford University Press, ISBN 978-0-19-929996-6(USA edition).

3) Trup, M. (n.d.). *Weave and Mend*. Song. arranged by Velma Frye.

4) Jermutus, M. (2011). *From Now to Now*. Leeds, Massachusetts: Pelorian Digital ISBN-13: 978-0615448930, ISBN-10: 0615448933. Page 273

5) Barnwell, Y. (n.d.). *We Are*. Song. arranged by Velma Frye.

Song Lyrics

I Come from Women (Amy Carol Webb)

I come from women who gave up their power. I come from women who gave up their name. And I come from women who know nothing ever stays the same.

I come from women tender as roses. I come from women strong as stone. And I come from women who know no one ever walks alone (who taught me no one ever fights alone).

I come from women who rocked their babies. I come from women who slept awake. And I come from women who guarded the fires for children's sake.

I come from women who vowed to do better. I come from women standing tall and strong. And I come from women who taught me I must always sing my song.

Chorus: Women of wisdom, women of tears, women who stood and embraced their fears. Women of struggle, women not free, women who passed the torch to me.

Bridge: So daughters everywhere raise fire high. Lift your voices to the sky. Mothers and sisters of the earth shout your name. Reclaim your worth. Now joining hands, we will be free.

Weave and Mend (Mary Trup)

Old woman is watching, watching over you. In the darkness of the storm she is watching. She is weaving, mending, gathering the fragments. She is watching over you.

Old woman is weaving, gathering the threads. Her bones become the loom she is weaving. She is watching, weaving, gathering the colors. She is watching over you.

For years I've been watching, waiting for old woman, feeling lost and so alone. I've been watching. Now I find her weaving, gathering the colors. Now I find her in myself.

Chorus: So weave and mend. Weave and mend. Gather the fragments, weave and mend the golden circles, sisters. Weave and mend. Weave and mend. Sacred sisters, weave and mend.

We Are (Ysaye Barnwell)

For each child that's born a morning star rises and sings to the universe who we are. (3 x)

We are our grandmother's prayers and we are our grandfather's dreams. We are the breath of the ancestors. We are the spirit of god. We are god. (3 x)

We are mothers of courage, fathers of time, daughters of dust, the sons of great visions, we're sisters of mercy, brothers of love, lovers of life, and builders of nations, we're seekers of truth, keepers of faith, makers of peace, the wisdom of ages. We are one.